SPOOKY
Indiana

Also in the Spooky Series by
S. E. Schlosser and Paul G. Hoffman:

SPOOKY
Indiana

Tales of Hauntings, Strange Happenings,
and Other Local Lore

RETOLD BY S. E. SCHLOSSER
ILLUSTRATED BY PAUL G. HOFFMAN

Guilford, Connecticut

Project editor: Meredith Dias
Layout: Justin Marciano
Text design: Lisa Reneson, Two Sisters Design
Map: Alena Pearce © Morris Book Publishing, LLC

Library of Congress Cataloging-in-Publication Data

Schlosser, S. E.
  Spooky Indiana : tales of hauntings, strange happenings, and other local
lore / retold by S.E. Schlosser ; illustrated by Paul G. Hoffman.
    p. cm.
  ISBN 978-0-7627-6421-1
  1. Ghosts—Indiana. 2. Haunted places—Indiana. I. Title.
  BF1472.U6S296 2012
  398.209772'05—dc23
                                              2012004544

Printed in the United States of America

For my family: David, Dena, Tim, Arlene, Hannah, Emma, Nathan, Ben, Deb, Gabe, Clare, Jack, Chris, Karen, Davey, and Aunt Mil. And for Barbara Strobel, an honorary member of the Schlosser clan.

For Erin Turner, Paul Hoffman, and all the wonderful folks at Globe Pequot Press, with my thanks.

For Jennifer White and for Jessica, Caleb, Jim, and Susan Smith. Thanks for all the great Indiana stories.

For Liz Reese, Bob Smith, and Zoe. Thanks for sharing your folks with me!

Contents

SPOOKY SITES . . . AND WHERE TO FIND THEM

Part One: Ghost Stories

1. Headlights - Bremen
2. Sophia - Hammond
3. The Purple Hand - Vincennes
4. The Chain - Orange County
5. Moody's Light - Francesville
6. Stiffy Green - Terre Haute
7. Ossian - Greencastle
8. The Lady in Black - Morgan-Monroe State Forest
9. The Face - Bloomington
10. Counterfeit - Leavenworth
11. Train Wreck - Hammond
12. Granny's Revenge - Peru

Part Two: Powers of Darkness and Light

13. Dog Face Bridge - San Pierre
14. Diamond Ring - Newburgh
15. Bloody Mary Whales - Lake County
16. The Dance - Miami County
17. Fireball - Huntington County
18. Loup-Garou - Evansville
19. Three Fawns - Shelby County
20. Tom Morgan's Dream - Jeffersonville
21. Strange Case - South Bend
22. Black Widow - La Porte
23. Reflection - Fort Wayne
24. The Night Shift - Indianapolis
25. Hatchet Man - Bloomington

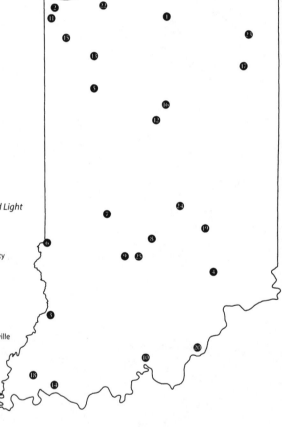

Contents

PART TWO: POWERS OF DARKNESS AND LIGHT

Introduction

The last vestiges of a storm brooded over Lake Michigan, turning the water into an endless series of whitecaps, on the final day of my *Spooky Indiana* research trip. I walked lazily down the steps from the parking lot and along the wood boardwalk that cut through the dunes. The wind whipped my hair into a mass of tangles, and I laughed as its chilly fingers caressed my cold cheeks. The beach in mid-afternoon—even on a cloudy day—was no place for shoes. I kicked them off and stepped down into the sand, catching them up with one hand as I headed toward the lake. The sand was cold against my bare feet; the wind took my breath away. Spray from the crashing waves misted the air like gentle rain. I saw a couple walking their golden retriever at the water's edge farther down the beach.

When I turned northward, I saw one, then two, then three crows fly in low over the dune and land near the water. Behind them, framing the scene, was the lighthouse at Michigan City—my first stop of the day and the last stop for the Hagenbeck-Wallace Circus before the fatal train wreck in 1918. Gulls farther up the beach huddled in a group near the base of the dune, uninterested in the crashing surf. But it was the crows I watched. They strutted closer to the crashing waves and then backed up quickly when the water came too close. I laughed again; it was as if they were playing.

Just then a jogger passed me, huddled into his sweatshirt as though he felt the cold in his bones. He didn't see the crows, didn't see me. I'm not even sure he registered the crashing waves as he ran along the shifting sand. The crows saw him, though, and flew away, sailing past me and landing farther down the beach, where they resumed their game of wave tag until the presence of the golden retriever persuaded them to head inland and out

of sight. I sighed and waved goodbye to the departing trio. Then I, too, headed inland to drive across the bridge at Cline Avenue in Hammond, which was haunted by the ghost of a jilted bride ("Sophia"), and to pay a quick visit to the phantom-plagued railroad tracks near Colfax Street, my last stop of the day before heading to the hotel to pack my bags for departure. Not that there would be much to see in daylight hours—at least at the railroad tracks. If and when a ghostly reenactment of the Hagenbeck-Wallace Circus train wreck happened, it would be in the wee hours of the morning, right around 3:57 a.m., the time the original accident took place ("Train Wreck"). Still, my spooky trip around Indiana would not be complete without a glimpse of the infamous site.

My adventures had begun two weeks earlier when I'd arrived in Goshen, my jumping off point for northern Indiana. I spent several days roaming through Amish country, enjoying homemade quilts and sweet treats, learning about life in the fertile farmlands, and visiting spooky spots like South Bend, where a grave robber met a terrible fate after stealing a dead woman's head for his phrenology studies ("Strange Case"). I paid a visit to the cemetery near Bremen, where ghostly headlights chase the unwary who venture there at night ("Headlights"). My visit to Fort Wayne produced the tale of a witch who still haunts the ruins of her house atop a hill ("Reflection"). Of course, the ghost of a bereaved farmer can still be seen wandering the fields between Francesville and Rensselaer ("Moody's Light").

After several wonderful days exploring the north, I headed down to Indianapolis, the source of many spooky tales. The one I chose for this collection involves a very haunted Central State Hospital ("The Night Shift"). Just a bit farther south is Bloomington, home to Indiana University and many spooky stories, including the infamous "Hatchet Man" and a certain ghostly young lady in a yellow dress ("The Face"). Farther west, the ghost of "Stiffy Green" wanders with his master through Terre Haute. Legend tells of three lovely witches who once roamed Shelby County in the shape of baby deer ("Three Fawns").

The final week of my journey took me through southern Indiana, where I found many tales of intrigue. In Jeffersonville, a murderer almost walked free, until the ghost of his victim appeared to a local man in a dream ("Tom Morgan's Dream"). A werewolf once preyed upon the townsfolk of Evansville ("Loup-Garou"). Counterfeiters used a cave near Leavenworth to print their false currency. And grave robbers in Newburgh accidentally saved the life of a grandmother who'd been buried alive when they dug up her casket to steal her diamond ring.

During the course of my stay in Indiana, I visited a revolving prison in Crawfordsville, spoke to many people who encountered ghosts in the normal course of their daily lives, laughed and cried over frontier tales of Daniel and Squire Boone and Abraham Lincoln, and made many friends. From the rolling hills and woodlands of southern Indiana to the dunes of Lake Michigan, Indiana is a state to remember. I hope you enjoy this glimpse of her spooky heritage.

—Sandy Schlosser

PART ONE
Ghost Stories

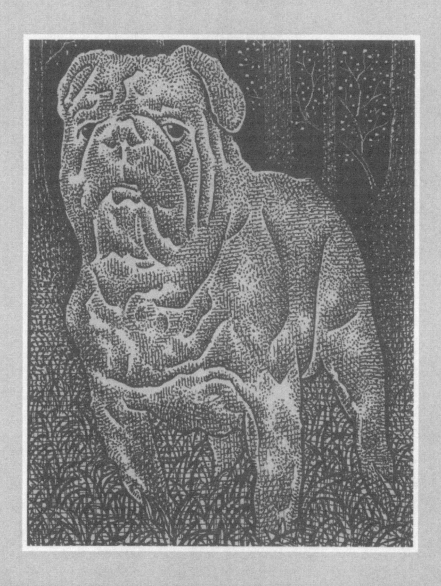

1

Headlights

I'd heard spooky stories about Little Egypt Cemetery all my life, and to be frank, I didn't believe any of them. Of course, fate, with its wicked sense of humor, made sure I fell in love with a true believer in ghosts to compensate for my skepticism. My wife-to-be knew all the stories about Little Egypt, and she took delight in repeating them around campfires and at family occasions.

Among her favorites was the tale of the girl who went parking with her boyfriend on the dirt road that circled around the cemetery. The boyfriend got out of the car to answer the call of nature and never returned. When the girl went to look for him, she found him hanging from a tree at the edge of the graveyard, a hand-braided rope around his neck. His ghost is said to haunt the tree where he died, and some of our friends claim they've seen the body of a man hanging from a tree in Little Egypt Cemetery on moonless nights.

According to another story, a quarter placed on a certain gravestone makes a phantom baby cry from beneath the ground where the child's grave-marker once stood. Apparently, the infant buried there choked to death on a quarter.

"That's just mean," I told my soon-to-be-wife the first time I heard the story. "That's reviving terrible memories for the poor kid."

"I thought you didn't believe in ghosts," my fiancée retorted.

"I don't," I said, "but you do, and I still think it's a mean thing to do."

My fiancée changed the subject, which was her tacit way of agreeing with me without saying so.

At a family barbecue a few days later, I overheard her relating a few more stories about Little Egypt Cemetery. Honestly, the place is so crowded with ghosts, it's a wonder there is any room left to bury anyone! This time, she told the story of a farmer who died in a nearby field. His ghost supposedly rises from the field and chases people out of the graveyard. In another story the ghost of a girl can be heard screaming in terror in the woods nearby. *Ha!* I thought. *The screamer was probably a real girl who'd scared herself silly telling ghost stories about Little Egypt!*

Then came the tale of the ghostly headlights. I blinked, not sure I'd heard my fiancée correctly. Haunted headlights? Surely she must be joking! I leaned my back against a nearby oak tree, trying to look inconspicuous, and listened a little closer.

"Route 5A makes a kind of square around the cemetery," my wife-to-be said to her breathless little cousins. "The phantom headlights appear as you are driving out of the cemetery. They come out of the woods and follow you down the road. Some people think it's the dead farmer chasing away people in his truck. Others say it is a malicious ghost trying to catch trespassers, and if the lights catch you before you get out of the cemetery, you'll never leave." She pitched her voice low and eerie as she uttered

HEADLIGHTS

the last phrase, and the little cousins shivered in unison as they shrieked in delighted terror.

"Hogwash!" I muttered, a little louder than I'd meant to.

"Don't you believe in ghosts?" asked a little cousin, her eyes wide with interest.

"Nope," I said, folding my arms across my chest and giving a decisive nod.

"He's just scared to try it," my fiancée said, giving me a wicked grin while the little cousins started chanting: "Fraidy-cat. Fraidy-cat."

I shook my head at their nonsense and strolled away to get another hamburger from the heavily packed food table.

About a week later, I was driving home after a night class when I happened to pass Hawthorne Road near the Little Egypt Cemetery. It was one of those silvery nights when the moon is almost full and the whole world seems full of mystery. I wasn't in any hurry to get home, and on impulse I headed down Hawthorne Road, suddenly curious to see Little Egypt Cemetery at nighttime. Grinning wolfishly, I turned onto the dirt road that leads around three-quarters of the cemetery before meandering through fields and woods to Gumwood Road. I could see the cemetery dead (pardon the pun!) ahead of me. The headstones were bright and clear in the moonlight, and they cast mysterious dark shadows in the black-and-white landscape. My headlights were on high beam and shone like strobes through the dark cemetery as I followed the curve to the left, beginning the bend around the perimeter. There, I could see a few sparse trees lining the wire fence. I assumed one of them must have been the tree involved in the alleged hanging, though I didn't see any hanging corpse illuminated by my high beams. I slowed around the next bend, still searching among the tombstones for a glowing farmer warning me off what was once his land. All I saw were moonlit fields with small, dark woods at the far end.

I touched the button to lower the passenger side window and slowed the car. Would I hear a baby cry? A girl scream? Nope. Nothing. Just the wind through the empty field . . . and the sudden rev of an engine!

Suddenly, a pair of burning white headlights appeared at the far edge of the field and roared out of the darkened wood heading straight toward the cemetery. My mouth dropped open in astonishment, and my heart started pounding. It wasn't possible for a car . . . or was it a truck? . . . to move that fast over a bumpy, harvested field. It had to be doing at least fifty, and it was speeding up! *It must be some crazy fool who delights in scaring sightseers away from Little Egypt,* I thought. Still, it made me tremble all over to see those lights coming closer, growing brighter. The vehicle roared louder than the combined noise of all the racecars in the Indianapolis 500, and my heart accelerated right with it.

It was strange that the high beams were all I could see of the vehicle, despite the bright moonlight. The lights raced toward me, getting brighter and brighter, and I realized the crazy fool driving the vehicle was heading right for the fence surrounding the cemetery. Then, the blinding lights came through the far side of the fence, and my heart leapt into my throat as I realized it wasn't a person driving that car! Or at least, not a living person! I gunned my own motor and raced around the next bend of the cemetery, the back end of my car skidding badly. I fought for control as the lights grew closer, dazzling my eyes until I could hardly see. I got the car back on the dirt road and slammed down on the gas as soon as I hit the straightaway. The phantom headlights burst through the near side of the cemetery fence, and the ghost vehicle came barreling after me at top speed.

The ghost car gained rapidly on me, and its headlights reflecting in my rearview mirror seemed as bright as the noonday sun. I pushed my foot hard on the gas pedal, but it was already touching the floor. I was well away from the cemetery already. Why was the ghost car still following me? It was on my tail and still accelerating. I was certain it was going to hit me. My hands were shaking so hard I could hardly keep them on the steering wheel. By then, the blazing white glare in my rearview and side mirrors was so bright that it nearly blinded me. Pressing pedal to the metal and praying I was still on the road, I braced myself for impact. The lights were a yard away, then a foot, then an inch . . . and then they were climbing up my bumper, glaring right through the back windshield, and rising toward the roof. I slammed my foot on the brakes as the lights traveled across the roof of the car and down over the front windshield. The whole car was shuddering and fighting, trying to spin out. The back end fishtailed as the lights glared blindingly right into my eyes. . . .

And disappeared.

I swore aloud in the sudden blackness and felt the car spin around in at least one complete 360. There may have been more. I took my foot off the brake and hung on for dear life, my eyes blind, save for the gray flashes that appeared every time I blinked. The car bumped over stubby field, slowed, and then stalled.

I collapsed against the steering wheel and tried to breathe. My heart was thundering so hard, it hurt my chest. I took panting breaths, trying to slow down my heart rate. I couldn't breathe deeply; my torso was too tight. I swayed a little, side to side, like a mother comforting her baby. *Come on, man. Get a grip!*

Slowly, my vision cleared, and I could see the lights of my dashboard. My head felt like it weighed a hundred pounds, but I managed to lift it and look out the window. I was only a couple yards off the road, out in some farmer's field. My car was facing back toward the cemetery. I could see a few of the taller gravestones illuminated in my high beams, which didn't look nearly so bright as they had when I'd first turned onto the dirt road.

It took three tries to get my car started again; my hands were trembling that bad. I carefully steered through the field and out onto the road, heading away from the cemetery. No way was I going back there! I drove slowly, like a little old man with bad eyesight, and nearly missed the turn onto Gumwood Road.

It took most of the drive home for my heart to settle back into its normal beat, and I was exhausted by the time I parked in my driveway. My trembling legs would barely hold me up when I stepped out of the car, and I leaned against the roof with my head bowed, at last able to take a couple of deep, calming breaths.

As I pushed myself upright, feeling old, I wondered what I should tell my fiancée. She'd believe me. Of course, she would. But did I want to spend the rest of my life being teased about my dramatic introduction to the reality of ghosts? I was too worn out to decide. I staggered into the house and went to bed. I'd decide in the morning.

2

Sophia

HAMMOND

The taxi driver was startled when a woman in white waved him down as he was driving into Hammond. Still, a fare was a fare. As he pulled up, he realized her fancy gown was, in fact, a wedding dress. The style was old-fashioned, but it looked good on her. She was young, with long blond hair and stunning blue eyes. *She must be a model on her way to a photography shoot,* the taxi driver thought admiringly. He couldn't think of any other reason why a lovely lady in a wedding gown should be hailing a taxi.

As the woman stepped into the back, the air in the taxi cooled abruptly, as if the driver has turned on the air conditioner—which he hadn't. The man shivered a little as he glanced in the rearview mirror and asked the lovely bridal figure for the address. She told him to drive to Cline Avenue in Hammond. The driver nodded and pulled out into traffic.

"You doing a photo shoot?" he asked, unable to control his curiosity.

At first, the woman did not answer. The taxi driver glanced into the rearview mirror, afraid he'd offended her with his question. When he saw her ashen face and trembling lips, he stuttered an apology.

The woman shook her head sadly. "No apology," she whispered. "The fault is not yours. It is mine. I thought . . . I thought . . ." Her voice drifted off on the last word, and she lifted a dainty hand and wiped her eyes.

The taxi driver tore his eyes away from the pale bride and kept them on the road as she told her story. . . .

She was seeing a man from the other side of town against her parent's wishes. They wanted her to marry a man from their own nationality, and her boyfriend came from another part of the world entirely. Still, the couple loved one another in spite of their differences, and they met often on the banks of the Calumet River. They planned to wed secretly, and she had saved all her money and bought the perfect wedding gown. On the appointed day, she snuck away after work to meet her boyfriend at a local church where a priest had agreed to marry them. She dressed herself carefully in her new wedding gown, and then she waited . . . and waited . . . and waited for her groom to arrive. But he never came. After two hours, the priest had gently urged her to return home, and she had reluctantly agreed.

"Oh miss, I'm so sorry," the taxi driver began, glancing in sympathy at the white-gowned woman pictured in the rearview mirror. Then he gasped! The woman in the backseat no longer wore a pristine white wedding gown. Now, she was soaked to the skin, her white wedding dress torn and covered in mud and river slime. Her face and lips were blue, and she seemed not to be breathing.

A desperately honking horn brought his attention back to the road. He'd swerved into the next lane while his attention was on the woman in the back, nearly causing an accident. The driver fought for control of the taxi and managed to get over to the side of the road just before the bridge over the Calumet River. He threw the taxi in park, put on his hazard lights, and whirled around to face the woman in the rear. The back seat was empty, except for a damp patch on the back seat and the smell of river water in the air.

The taxi driver clutched at his heart in shock. What? How? He fell back against the seat and took long, slow breaths, trying to calm himself. Then he put on his blinker and pulled back into traffic, wondering what the heck had just happened to him.

He thought about the eerie incident the rest of the day. Finally, he told one of his friends about the incident. His buddy, who had been driving a taxi in Hammond for a long time, didn't seem surprised by the story.

"Did she ask you to take her to Cline?" he asked.

"How'd you know?" the taxi driver asked in astonishment.

"That was Sophia," his buddy said. "She's been haunting that stretch of highway for a long time. She didn't tell you the end of her story. The day her boyfriend left her waiting at the church, she ran outside and hailed a cab to take her home. But when they reached the stretch of Cline Avenue near the bridge, she told the taxi driver to halt. Then, she leapt out of the cab, raced frantically down to the edge of the water, and threw herself into the river before the cab driver could stop her. Her heavy skirts pulled her underwater, and she was swept away by the current. Some fishermen found her body a few days later, floating along the shore in her ruined wedding gown."

The taxi driver shook his head in sorrow, remembering the tears the woman in white had shed in his back seat.

"Poor girl," he murmured. "Poor abandoned girl."

SOPHIA

"They say her fiancé was killed in a mill accident the day before the wedding. That's why he didn't show," his buddy said.

"Did anyone ever tell Sophia that?" asked the taxi driver. "Maybe it would help her to rest in peace."

"You do that, the next time she asks you for a ride," his buddy said, half in jest.

"Maybe I will," said the taxi driver. But remembering the drowned figure in his back seat, he wasn't so sure he wanted to give Sophia another ride in his taxi. Once was enough.

3

The Purple Hand

VINCENNES

I got my first job in town back in 1895, the year I turned fourteen. Pa was doing poorly that year, and we needed the money to help supplement the family income from what Pa and Ma raised on the farm, which wasn't too much that year on account of Pa's health. So I dropped out of school, worked in the fields during the mornings, and spent my afternoons and evenings doing odd jobs at the sawmill.

We lived a fair piece out of town, so I rode the horse back and forth to work whenever I wasn't needed on the farm. When Pa needed the horse to plow or do other chores, I'd walk to town, and Pa would pick me up in the wagon when I was done in the evening. It gave him a chance to sit with the other farmers in the mercantile and play checkers while I finished work.

A few weeks after I started my job at the mill, I had to stay late on the farm to help Pa untangle the bull from a wire fence in which he'd trapped himself trying to get a piece of choice grass on the far side. It was tricky work pulling out the bull without injuring him further on the sharp barbs, and by the time we'd freed the critter, it was past time for me to be gone. I was a-feared of losing my new job when we needed the money so bad, and so I did a stupid thing. I took the shortcut to town over the railroad bridge that crossed the Wabash River near the haunted battlefield.

Pa and Ma had both forbidden me to go near the spot because of the haunts, but it was an emergency. Besides, it was broad daylight. So I turned off the main road and cantered along the railroad tracks, carefully crossing the bridge after making sure no trains were in sight. It was a peaceful ride, kind of pretty with the Wabash murmuring under the bridge and the trees shading the banks.

I got to work on time and made a mental note to use the shortcut if ever I was late again. As I loaded logs and stacked timber, I got to wondering why my folks had made such a fuss about that part of the river. They'd never told me much about it beyond mentioning a battle during the French and Indian War, and that it was haunted. So I asked my employer, Mr. Smith, about the story during my dinner break.

"It was a nasty time, hereabouts," Mr. Smith said, leaning against the wall of the mill and lighting his pipe. "This was the far edge of the frontier back in the early days of this century, and the natives didn't like the white settlers taking their land. Skirmishes took place every week, but the fight on the Wabash was an out-and-out battle between the white folks and the Indians. It took place during the spring floods, and the river roared and foamed in the background as guns blazed, tomahawks whirled, and spears and knives flew every which way. Warriors were whooping, and men were shouting defiance or screaming in agony. Blood was everywhere, littering the ground and coloring the floodwaters."

I leaned forward, eagerly taking in every word.

Mr. Smith puffed thoughtfully on his pipe and then continued: "The story goes that a brave medicine man had followed his chief into battle and was killed at the tail end of the skirmish, just as his chief achieved victory over the encroaching settlers. The medicine man's body was flung from his horse and toppled into the floodwaters of the Wabash, right at the spot where the railroad bridge now stands. Horrified, the warriors swarmed the banks of the river, trying to rescue the body of their friend and holy man. But his body was swept away in the raging river and was never found."

Mr. Smith paused and drew on his pipe. I fidgeted impatiently on the bench, willing him to go on.

"Now, you must understand, Joseph, that in the traditions of this particular tribe, a soul cannot move on to the next world unless the body has had a proper burial. So the soul of the medicine man was bound to the place where he was killed, tied forever to the river in that place."

Mr. Smith lowered his voice and intoned in a sepulchral manner, "Those who linger too long in that locale will see him rising in despair from the waters of the Wabash, unable to rest until his body is found."

The air around me suddenly seemed chilly. I felt goose bumps rising on my arms, and I jumped up quickly to hide my nervousness.

"Better get back to work," I gabbled, my voice pitched higher than normal.

Mr. Smith laughed at my fright. Then, half-laughing and totally serious, he told me to stay away from that part of the Wabash.

I took the long way home that night and in the days and weeks that followed. I didn't consciously avoid the haunted place on the riverbank by the railroad bridge, but somehow I never had the urge to take the shortcut.

Late one evening in August as I was finishing my work at the sawmill, Jimmy Hinks, the local doctor's eldest son, came trotting up on his horse. He was out of breath and upset. As soon as I saw him I knew something was wrong at home. Mr. Smith knew it, too. He came out of the office and gripped my shoulder as Jimmy slid down from the horse.

"Joseph!" he called out. "Your Pa's had an accident. Cut his leg real bad with the axe. He lost a lot of blood before your Ma found him. My father's on his way, and he sent me to fetch you home."

"Go on, son. I'll finish up here," Mr. Smith said, giving my shoulder a squeeze.

I nodded to my boss, thanked Jimmy, and quickly saddled my horse. I jumped on and rode as fast as I could go—aiming, without thinking, for the shortcut over the railroad bridge. The sun was setting in a blaze behind the sawmill as I rode for the river. A moment later, the sun was gone, leaving behind a sleepy dusk full of chirping birds and crickets and the pounding of my horse's hooves. The wind whistled around me as I rode, and darkness came quickly now that the sun had set.

As I came to the trees along the riverbank, the shadows deepened. I slowed my horse, realizing that it would be doubly hard on my mother if both Pa and I had accidents on the same day. *Make haste carefully,* I told myself as we came up to the railroad tracks. I glanced both ways. There was no train in sight. I turned my horse onto the bridge, and the wind came whipping along between the banks and blew the hair away from my forehead.

THE PURPLE HAND

My thoughts were all on my Pa, so I wasn't prepared for the light that sprang up suddenly from the water to the right of the bridge. My horse whinnied and shied. I reined him in, my eyes fixed on the strange white light. The water was eddying beneath the glow, and suddenly a purple hand burst out of the depths of the river. My eyes popped and my heart thudded heavily against my ribs as the hand stretched upward, fingers splayed, as if someone just beneath the surface were reaching desperately for help.

My horse took a few uneasy steps to the side, away from the glowing hand beneath us, and rolled his eyes in fear. I kept a tight grip on him as a long purple arm followed the hand upward, and then a ghastly, bloated purple face appeared in the swirling water underneath the arm. Lurid green light glowed within its eye sockets, and long black hair tangled around the face like swaying seaweed. The purple lips were torn, as if they had been dragged across sharp rocks, and the face was so swollen it no longer looked human.

The loathsome head continued to rise above the water as I stared in frozen horror. Then, a bolt of sheer, blinding terror blazed through my body like streaked lightning as my brain finally registered what my eyes were seeing. A phantom was rising from the water just a few paces from the place where I sat on my horse! I really didn't want to know what it would do once its body was free of the river.

With a scream of sheer terror, I kneed my shying horse, and we bolted across the railroad bridge, our faces illuminated by crisscrossing rays of purple, green, and white light that were shining up through the gaps in the wood. Above the pounding of hooves, I thought I heard an anguished moan from the middle of the river, but I dared not look back. I just concentrated on staying in the saddle as tree branches whipped my face and my horse did his best to win a speed record for cross-country sprinting.

In record time, we raced into our farmyard, and the horse bolted for the safety of the barn. I threw myself off just in time to avoid decapitation as he raced through the low side door meant solely for human entry. I rolled as I hit the ground, like Pa had taught me, thus preventing broken bones—though I'd have some spectacular bruises. I lay for a moment, stomach heaving with fear and loathing, the bloated purple face still glowing behind my eyelids. What a terrible fate, to be tied to one place, unable to rest in peace.

Then I remembered my Pa and leapt up, my feet barely touching the ground as I raced inside the house. Pa was lying on the bed with a big, white bandage around his lower left leg. The doctor was sitting beside him drinking tea, and Ma was bustling about making Pa comfortable. They all looked up when I burst in, and I could tell from the look on Ma's face that the accident was not nearly as bad as she'd feared.

"I'm all right, son," Pa said quickly, seeing my pale face and shaking body. "It's just a flesh wound."

Ma came up and put her arms around me comfortingly.

"He's got to stay off that leg for a week or two and keep the wound clean," the doctor said. "But he should be just fine."

I sagged with relief. Then, Ma made me a cup of tea and sat me down beside the bed to drink it while she took care of my horse.

Mr. Smith generously gave me time off to work on the farm while Pa recuperated. As the doctor predicted, Pa was back on his feet in two weeks, and I was back at the sawmill working the evening shift by the end of the month. But I was careful to ride the long way around after that night. I was done with purple hands.

4

The Chain

ORANGE COUNTY

I was visiting my cousin's farm in the spring of 1935 while I conducted some business in a nearby town. At the dinner table the first evening, I mentioned my intention to visit Bonds Chapel Cemetery the next day to pay my respects at the grave of my great-aunt.

"Mother spoke of her fondly," I told my cousin Jonathan. "She asked me to place flowers on Great Aunt Celia's grave while I was visiting here."

Jonathan looked grim. "I wouldn't do that if I were you, Robert," he said. "I have heard some strange stories about Bonds Chapel Cemetery."

I couldn't restrain my smirk. Jonathan and his wife, Frances, were spiritualists and fond of table turning, séances, and rot like that. I should have known better than to mention my plan to visit the graveyard.

Frances leaned toward me across the table and said earnestly: "The ghost of a logger haunts the cemetery." She studied the look of disbelief on my face and nodded solemnly. "It's true! According to the story, the logger came home from work one evening and found his wife with another man. In a fit of rage, he strangled her with his logging chain and hid the body, and then he claimed she ran away with her lover. But the dying wife put a curse on her murderous husband, and her vengeance followed swiftly. A few days after the murder, a chain broke loose from a timber wagon on which the logger was working. It came whipping through the air and snapped the man's neck. They say it was the very same logging chain he'd used to kill his wife!"

Jonathan took up the tale from his place at the head of the table. "The logger was buried in Bonds Chapel Cemetery, and a year to the day after his death, a chain began forming on his tombstone. Year after year, more links appeared until they formed a cross on the side of the tomb. They say that anyone who touches the chain on the tombstone will die by the chain, just as the logger did."

"Sometimes, the logger's ghost is seen rising from the graveyard at night," Francis added. "His wife's curse has followed him beyond the grave, and he cannot rest as long as the chain remains upon his tombstone."

It was not easy, but I managed to keep my face straight during their earnest recitation of the logger-ghost story. I knew Jonathan and Frances truly believed in ghosts and curses and were trying to warn me out of the goodness of their hearts. But the whole thing made me want to laugh.

I took a long drink of water to restore myself. I thanked them gravely for the warning and assured them I would visit the cemetery only during daylight hours and would not go near the logger's grave. Then, I excused myself from the table and waited until my bedroom door was firmly shut before I gave way to the mirth I'd been holding in during dinner.

I'd meant to keep my promise to my cousins . . . truly. But business kept me overlong in town the next day, and it was dusk before I turned my brand new Auburn 851 Supercharged Boattail Speedster toward my cousin's farm, located several miles out of town. The Auburn was a beautiful sports car, and it was a beautiful evening for a drive, so I put down the top and decided to take a detour to the cemetery to pay my respects to my great-aunt, just like I'd promised Mother. I stopped by the side of the road, picked a nice bunch of wildflowers to lay on my great-aunt's grave, and drove to Bonds Chapel.

An eerie twilight lay over the cemetery as I parked my car on the outskirts and picked up the impromptu bouquet. It was almost too dark to read the headstones, so I hurried back to the car and turned on the headlights, which made the shadows appear darker and more ominous. It was hard to see anything outside the lights, and my imagination populated the surrounding darkness with evil spirits full of dark menace.

"Poppycock," I muttered to reassure myself. I was getting as fanciful as Jonathan and Frances.

The temperature dropped dramatically as I entered the cemetery for the second time. The flowers in my hand drooped from the cold. Shivering, I told myself to buck up. I was letting my cousins' stories affect my imagination. But that didn't prevent me from walking rapidly up and down, scanning tombstones for my Great Aunt Celia.

Just as I turned away from a crumbling obelisk marking the tomb of a man who'd died at the advanced age of eighty-seven, I saw a chain marking a gravestone a few yards away. It was a strange-looking object. It didn't look as if it had been put there at the behest of the family. No, the chain looked as if it had

THE CHAIN

formed itself on the headstone. In fact, when I peered closer, I saw there were two chains, one vertical and one horizontal, that formed the shape of a cross.

Gooseflesh rose on my arms as I remembered the story of the logger. I took an involuntary step backward and almost screamed when I bumped into a tombstone behind me. It was pitch-black all around me, except for the too-bright headlights of the Auburn. The whole cemetery had gone silent. No chirping crickets, no soughing wind, no rustle of night creatures through the grass. No sound at all.

I shuddered, and the flowers slipped out of my shaking hands. I decided it would be better to return in daylight to look for my great-aunt's grave. I turned quickly toward my car, forcing myself to saunter even though I wanted to run.

Suddenly, all the shadows disappeared in front of me in a blaze of white light. For a split second, I stared blankly at the huge dark shadow cast by my own body. Then, I whirled around and saw a white mist rising from the ground beneath the gravestone with the chain on it. The mist glowed brighter than my headlights. It was forming into the figure of a man. I shrieked, spun back around, tripped over the small tombstone of a baby, righted myself, and sprinted for my car. The light behind me grew brighter, and the air around me grew so cold that my desperate, panting breaths turned to fog in front of my face as I ran.

Fortunately for me, the top was down on my Auburn, and I vaulted into the driver's seat without opening the door and got the car started on the first try. I turned the car around fast and raced away from the cemetery, darting a quick look back at the glowing figure hovering menacingly a few feet above the tombstones. I turned my head back around just in time to see a thick logger's chain hanging at head-height between two trees. I shouted and ducked simultaneously, hitting the brakes. The chain ripped right through the windshield, bending the metal and shattering the window. Glass cascaded all over me as the car shuddered to a halt. I sat up, pop-eyed, and saw a glowing figure shooting toward me in the rear-view mirror. I hit the gas and drove away as fast as I could, bleeding from numerous glass cuts on my scalp, neck, and back. The broken glass of the windshield shimmered around me like tiny stars in the fading light of the phantom, which was left far behind.

The drive home was a blur. One moment I was driving frantically away from a glowing figure, and the next minute I was parking beside my cousin's barn. I was a mess. My car was a mess.

When my cousins heard the Austin roar into their yard, they came running out of the house with a lantern. When they saw the ruined car, they exclaimed in alarm. I stumbled out of the driver's seat and fell at Jonathan's feet. Francis started crying when she saw the blood trickling down my face and covering my clothes. They hustled me into the house and wouldn't listen to a word until I was cleaned up and bandaged. To their credit, they did not chide me for not heeding their warning about the ghost. Francis clucked and sympathized while Jonathan handed me a stiff brandy.

"We'll take you to visit your great-aunt's grave tomorrow," Jonathan said as I downed the drink in one gulp.

I choked, sputtered, swallowed hard, and said, "No thanks! I'll let you represent Mother. I've had enough graveyards for one visit. I only wish I could get that phantom to pay for the car repairs!"

"Just be thankful you still have your head," Jonathan said dryly. "If you'd have touched that gravestone, you probably wouldn't be sitting here talking to me."

I stared at him, wide-eyed. I'd forgotten about the curse on the gravestone. The fact that I hadn't touched the marker may very well have explained the miraculous way I'd turned just in time to see the logging chain and duck out of the way before it chopped through my windshield. I clutched at my neck, and my stomach lurched unhappily.

"Enough, Jonathan," Francis said. "Robert needs to rest."

I sure did. It was bad enough to find out ghosts did exist, even worse to have one try to kill me. I wasn't sure my nerves could take anything else. I got shakily to my feet and headed to my bedroom. This time, I wasn't laughing, and I sure as heck wasn't going back to Bonds Chapel Cemetery!

5

Moody's Light

FRANCESVILLE

Only the light remains now . . . Moody's light . . . a silent token of an unspeakable tragedy. I wish the light would disappear so I, for one, could forget the story. But legends have a way of sticking around, even when they are not wanted. So the stories continue to swirl around the neighborhood, as folks try to explain away the ghost light that wanders through the fields between Francesville and Rensselaer. Of course, only a few ever knew the real tale, and now I am the only one still alive who was there when it happened.

Moody was my neighbor, you see, back in those days. He was a pleasant, round-faced fellow with a charming, plump wife and winsome twin daughters. The elder twin was fair and plump like her mother. The other twin had long auburn curls and an oval face. She did not resemble either of her parents, but folks said she looked like her maternal great-aunt.

Moody worked hard on his farm, trying to set aside enough money to send his two girls to a posh boarding school in the city, the kind usually reserved for rich girls and the daughters of European nobles. Moody's girls were really smart. He wanted them to have a good education, and he was sure they could hold

their own against any rich girl in the country. His wife agreed
with him, although I believe she was more interested in having
them meet eligible young men than in getting a fancy degree
from a private high school.

Late one afternoon in early August, Moody dropped in at
my farm with his face aglow with excitement. He was on his way
home from the post office, where he'd picked up an acceptance
letter from the boarding school. His girls were in! He shook my
hand heartily, as if I were the one who'd won admittance to the
school, and he gave my wife, Mildred, a big kiss on the cheek
before waltzing his way out into our yard, eager to get home and
share the good news with his family. I glanced askance at Mildred
when he left, wondering why Moody had told us the good news
before telling his family. Of course, our farm lay on his route
home. Maybe he couldn't wait any longer to share his news.

I was out in the barn tending a festering sore on the leg of
one of my milk cows when I heard an agonized scream from
the direction of Moody's farm. My head jerked up and my hand
slipped, wiping medicated cream down the leg of my cow. I
heard a second scream and leapt off my stool, leaving behind
my confused, half-tended beast as I sprang out the barn door.

I ran to the house, grabbed my rifle from the rack, and raced
toward the farm with my wife, carrying our spare rifle, right
behind me. Millie is as good a shot as I am, and I was glad to
have her backing me up as I ran to the rescue of Moody and his
family. I could only imagine the reason for the alarm—perhaps
a wild animal attack or some terrible accident. I could still hear
screaming and could tell it was a man. It sounded like Moody.

As Millie and I raced down the road between our two farms,
I half-expected to meet up with one of Moody's daughters or his

wife, come to fetch us for help, but no one came. We ran across the farmyard toward the sound of the screams and a moment later found Moody on his knees in the back yard, bloody hands pressed over his eyes. He was rocking back and forth in agony, and the body of his charming, plump wife lay before him. She was quite dead, her chest ripped open as if she'd been attacked by a wild beast. But the wounds were too straight to be claw marks, my hunter's eye told me after a moment's observation. She'd been stabbed to death, and the killer had ripped out her heart. The blood was mostly dry, so the murder had happened several hours ago.

Millie stood gasping behind me. After a horrified moment, she cried, "The girls! Moody, where are the girls?"

Moody lifted his face out of his hands and stared at her blankly. My heart slammed against my ribs in sudden apprehension.

"You stay here," I ordered my wife. "Your gun is loaded? Good. Keep the safety off."

Millie nodded and took up a guard stance over Moody. I gulped, not wanting to move, and then forced myself to enter the house. The metallic stench of blood nearly overwhelmed me as I stepped into the kitchen. Gore streaked over the walls, the floor, and down the center of the large wooden table. Bloody footprints led toward the front room. The shoe size was at least two sizes smaller than Moody's big feet, I noticed dispassionately, as I tried to keep my dinner down.

I followed the footprints into the parlor, which had been torn to bits, furniture overturned, glass littering the floor from the broken picture frames and cracked lantern globes. The bloody footsteps turned the corner and led upstairs. I followed them, holding my rifle ready to fire. At the top of the stairs, the footsteps led into the first bedroom.

MOODY'S LIGHT

Taking a deep breath, I stepped inside and yelled in horror. I couldn't help it. The head of the older twin was staring lifelessly at me from on top of the closest bedpost, her face screwed up into a rictus of terror. Her body was strewn across the dressing table like a discarded towel. The younger sister was curled in the fetal position on the bed, her chest as bloody as her mother's, her young heart removed from its protective ribbing. My stomach overruled my head, and I threw up on the floor at the foot of the bed, right beneath the elder daughter's head.

I heard Millie's footsteps pounding up the stairs, but I was too ill to shout at her to stay where she was. A moment later, she was in the doorway and immediately turned aside and vomited in the hallway.

"Get the sheriff," I gasped to her. "Take the horse. Hurry! I'll watch over Moody."

As Millie straightened, she wiped her mouth on her sleeve. Then she ran shakily downstairs and out to Moody's barn. Within minutes, I heard her racing up the road, riding one of the plow horses bareback. I went downstairs and outside to Moody. As I strode through the devastated front parlor, I saw an envelope lying forgotten on the floor. It was the acceptance letter from the posh boarding school.

I stood guard over Moody, knowing he would be considered a suspect by the sheriff—at least until he saw the bloody footprints. I don't know how long we waited there, with Moody moaning beside his dead wife and me staring at nothing, trying to go numb, trying not to feel.

The sheriff and his men combed the house, pastures, and surrounding countryside looking for the killer. Aside from the bloody footprints, there was no other clue to his identity. The footprints cleared Moody, and the sheriff sent the dazed farmer home with my wife and me while they searched his house for clues and then cleaned up as much of the devastation as they could. The coroner took the bodies to the morgue, and my wife made arrangements for the funeral.

Poor Moody couldn't speak for days following the tragedy. He stuttered his way through the sheriff's initial interrogation, but then stopped speaking altogether, save for answering a simple yes or no to questions. He didn't snap out of it until after the funeral, when the sheriff stopped by our farm to tell us he'd heard tell of a gang of ruffians roaming the area looking for innocent females to harass. The sheriff thought one or more of the gang had probably murdered Moody's family. The news snapped Moody out of his shock. Now, he had something concrete to fix his attention on. He was determined to find the man or men who'd killed his family and bring them to justice.

The next few months, the only time I saw Moody was when he wandered past our house with his rifle, searching the highways and byways, the pasturelands, and the open fields for the ruffians who'd murdered his family. I swear he checked under every haystack and through every row of corn. After a few weeks, his anger cooled some. By the time the sheriff called off the search, Moody seemed resigned to the verdict of "death by person or persons unknown."

Still, he continued to roam the fields each night after dark. Long after good folk were in bed, I'd see the glow of Moody's lantern out in the pastures. Millie and I were sure he wasn't eating properly. Every time we saw him, he looked thinner and more unkempt—unshaven, wild-eyed, his clothing tattered and threadbare. When I looked into his eyes, I saw a shattered man who had lost everything he cared about in this world. I saw him less and less during the day, but his lantern always roamed the fields at night.

Toward Christmas, Millie and I went to visit my ailing mother. We were away for nearly a month. When we got home, the sheriff stopped in to give us the news. He'd sent a deputy over to Moody's place to check up on the farmer, since he hadn't been seen in town for more than a week. The deputy found his body hanging from a tree near the barn. Suicide.

When the sheriff left, Millie got up and walked over to the window to stare down the lane toward Moody's place. I could tell she had something on her mind and waited for her to come out with it.

"Honey, I need to tell you something," she said after a long silence. "I swore to Mrs. Moody that I'd never say a word about the matter while her husband was alive, and I've kept that promise."

My heart thundered against my ribs. *This is it,* I thought, *the missing piece to the story.* Perhaps Millie's secret would help make sense of this terrible, unsolved mystery.

Millie drew in a deep breath and then said: "Moody wasn't the father of the twins. His wife had an affair with a man who was passing through several years back. She didn't say who it was, and I didn't ask. Anyway, she ended the affair before the twins were born, and Moody never guessed that his wife had been unfaithful."

She sat down suddenly on a chair and sagged with relief. The truth must have weighed on her a great deal over the years. I wondered how long ago Mrs. Moody had spoken to her. I studied Millie's face and realized there was more.

"And?" I prompted softly after the silence had stretched on a few seconds too long.

Millie hesitated. Then she said: "I heard that a man with curly, auburn hair and an oval face passed through town right around the time of the murders. The counter girl at the mercantile thought he might be related to the Moody family because he looked so much like the younger daughter. I thought maybe . . ."

"You thought he might be the man Mrs. Moody had the affair with?" I guessed. "That he was the one who killed her and the twins? He came back through town, saw the girls, and guessed the truth?"

"It was all hearsay," Millie said wretchedly. "Mrs. Moody never told me the man's name. And I couldn't accuse a man of murder just because he had auburn hair and was passing through town the day the murders took place. I never saw the man myself. I had only the counter girl's description to go by. And she didn't know his name or anything about him, except that he'd stopped at the store to buy tobacco. And, of course, I'd promised Mrs. Moody I wouldn't say anything about the girls."

Millie paused for a moment and then added, "Besides, I'm not so sure it was him. And I don't think the girls went to town that day."

My heart sank suddenly, anticipating her. No, the girls hadn't gone to town that day. But Moody had gone to town, hoping the acceptance letter would arrive. He might have seen the man at the store and guessed who he was. He'd had plenty of time to go home, confront his wife with the truth, clean himself up afterward, and walk over to our farm to show us the acceptance letter. His presence in our house at the time would make a good alibi. I had thought it strange that he should have stopped by to tell Millie and me the news before he'd told his own family, but I'd forgotten all about my uneasiness during the trauma that followed. Of course, there were the too-small-for-Moody footprints to account for. But Moody could have used any old pair of boots dipped in blood to make those oh-so-handy footprints.

Millie saw the look on my face and said hastily, "I'm probably wrong. We will never really know, will we?"

I shook my head—not in denial of her statement but in sorrow. It was a tragedy, whatever the truth of the matter.

We spoke about the situation a while longer and decided to confide the story to the sheriff, in case he wanted to follow up on the red-haired stranger. But nothing came out of the lead—at least nothing I ever heard. The triple murder remained an unsolved mystery.

Millie and I had hoped to forget the tragedy, but Moody's ghost light appeared in the fields the very night we got home from my mother's house and learned of his suicide. We've seen it regularly ever since then.

Moody's farm is gone now. The only thing left is the light . . . and the stories, which have become so garbled that no one knows the truth. Not even me.

Rest in peace, Moody.

6

TERRE HAUTE

The year I turned seven, both of my parents died in a carriage accident, and I moved in with my grandparents. I had been in my new home for only a week when I first visited the floral shop and met old Mr. Heinl. I had to step down as I entered the shop, which took me by surprise. I almost fell on my face, and while I regained my balance, the little bell jingled overhead and the door swung wide. When I was more or less back on my feet, I looked around and stopped abruptly in amazement, my mouth dropping open. My nose was assailed by various floral scents, and an amazing array of colors met my eyes. I'd never seen so many flowers in one place before. Behind me, Granddaddy chuckled and urged me forward as he closed the door behind us.

I walked around, wide-eyed, exploring every aisle, touching a smooth petal here, sniffing a rose there. The place was full of bright flowers as well as ferns and plants I'd never seen before. There were even a few small trees! At last, I came to the back of the store, where Granddaddy sat talking to a gregarious old man who was puffing on a pipe, and I spotted a big bulldog snoozing behind the counter. I loved dogs and wanted to pet him, but the old man—Mr. Heinl—said that Stiffy Green didn't much like people, so I left him alone. To ease my disappointment, old Johnny Heinl gave me a peppermint to eat while he and granddaddy talked. It was the first of many sweets I received from Mr. Heinl.

As I rolled the peppermint around in my mouth, I studied the bulldog. *Stiffy Green is a funny name*, I thought, and so I asked Mr. Heinl about it. Chuckling, he said it was because the old bulldog walked with a stiff gait and had piercing green eyes. "Huh," I said, not knowing what else to say.

I held out my hand toward Stiffy Green. The bulldog raised his head, looked me up and down, and then came over to be stroked.

"He likes you," old John Heinl said in surprise.

And so he did. Stiffy Green was a rugged fellow who adored his master and didn't much care for anyone else. But from that day on, we were friends. He'd let me and my granddaddy pet him, which was quite an honor. We were practically the only people he tolerated aside from his master. Sometimes, the old dog would consent to romp with me in the yard behind the floral shop.

Granddaddy said Mr. Heinl would have been very lonely if he didn't have Stiffy Green. Mrs. Heinl had passed away several years before, and now the only one Mr. Heinl had to keep him company in his rambling old house was Stiffy Green. The bulldog slept every night beside his master's bed, guarding him from harm. The two were inseparable.

The old man and his old bull dog loved to walk around town in the evenings after they closed up the floral shop. Mr. Heinl carried his walking stick and puffed on his pipe, while

STIFFY GREEN

Stiffy Green trotted beside him, pausing here and there to sniff an interesting smell. Mr. Heinl would nod to folks and call out a greeting, and they would respond with a smile and a wave. Everyone in town loved John Heinl, but few dared to approach the man when he was out walking with his dog. Stiffy Green greeted people with a glare and a growl, for he was very protective of his master. He put aside his gruff manner only when he passed my grandparents' house and saw me playing in the yard. Then, he would trot over and romp with me while Granddaddy talked to Mr. Heinl.

About a year after I moved to Terre Haute, old Mr. Heinl passed away in his sleep with Stiffy Green on guard beside him. It was very sad. I went to the funeral with my grandparents, and we brought Stiffy Green with us. The big bulldog sat mournfully through the service and watched with us as his beloved master's casket was interred in the Heinl family mausoleum. After the gate around the mausoleum was locked, we took Stiffy Green over to John Heinl's cousin, who had agreed to give the aged bulldog a home. I hugged the big, old dog fiercely, tears running down my cheeks.

As we left the cemetery, I saw Stiffy Green trot back over to the fence surrounding the mausoleum, refusing to leave his master. I heard later that they had to tie him up with a rope and drag him along to the cousin's house that night. But Stiffy Green wouldn't stay there. He'd gnaw and gnaw at the rope until it broke, and then he would gallop over to the cemetery to stand guard over his master's tomb.

After several attempts to keep him at home, the cousin gave up, and Stiffy Green moved into the graveyard permanently. The staff made a shelter for him behind the mausoleum and fed him tidbits from their lunches. My grandma sent me over with food for my old canine friend several times a week. Stiffy Green was always happy to see me, but he never would stray far from John Heinl's tomb.

As the months passed, Stiffy Green lived up to his name, and as his gait grew increasingly stiffer, his inclination to move steadily declined, too. I knew he was ready to join his master.

The cemetery workers sent us word when Stiffy Green passed on. My grandfather and several of John Heinl's friends met to discuss what to do about his faithful companion. They decided his body should be stuffed and mounted and laid to rest in the mausoleum beside his master. I didn't favor the idea myself. It seemed a bit gruesome to me, but I didn't get a vote in the matter.

It soon became a popular pastime for the children at my school to peak through the windows of the mausoleum to see Stiffy Green still on guard beside his master's body. I never went there, even when my buddies begged me to come along. I thought it would spoil my memory of the old bulldog.

One evening about two months after Stiffy Green's death, I was walking home past the cemetery at dusk when I heard a dog barking inside the fence. My heart skipped a beat, for it sounded just like the bark Stiffy Green used to give when he saw me coming to play with him. I looked around, wondering if my grandparents had been mistaken and Stiffy Green were still alive. Then, I saw the old bulldog barreling toward me among the gravestones. "Stiffy!" I shouted, running forward and swinging myself up and over the fence. I knelt to hug my buddy, and my arms went right through him. Gasping, I sat back as a translucent tongue tried to wash my face and eager paws alighted on my shoulders. A cold, clammy mist seeped through my clothes where the ghost dog touched me. As I stared into glowing green eyes as eager and young as a puppy's eyes, I couldn't be afraid.

Someone whistled behind me. Stiffy Green shook himself, gave my cheek a final freezing-cold lick, and trotted off. I whirled and saw old John Heinl strolling down the path leading to the mausoleum, pipe in one hand, walking stick in the other. He nodded and waved to me as Stiffy Green joined him, tail wagging. I waved back, my mouth open in shock. They both vanished as twilight stillness settled over the cemetery.

I sat there for a long time, thinking about what I'd seen. Finally, I stood up and grinned. The ache I'd felt in my chest whenever I'd thought about John Heinl and Stiffy Green was gone, never to return. Something else happened, too. I reasoned that, if old Mr. Heinl and his dog were still around, maybe my dead parents weren't far away, either. With a lighter heart, I vaulted the cemetery fence and ran home to supper with my grandparents.

7

Ossian

GREENCASTLE

Teddy was bored. He had a history exam tomorrow but couldn't concentrate on his books. He'd been studying for days, and all the facts and figures swirling around in his brain no longer made any sense. In frustration, he slammed his books shut and piled them under his arm. A change of scene might help him concentrate.

Teddy threw the history books into his rucksack and headed down the street to the campus library. Along the way, he nodded greetings to several acquaintances, ogled the pretty daughter of the dean, and spent a half hour commiserating with his fellow history students over the upcoming test.

By the time he entered the library building, Teddy was feeling much better. He chose a spot near Governor James Whitcomb's rare-book collection, which had been recently donated to the library, and settled there with his history books. He'd browsed the governor's collection a time or two and found some interesting reading material therein. Unfortunately, none of the books were eligible for circulation, so Teddy was forced to read them in his leisure time—which, at the moment, was nonexistent. Still, when history got overwhelming, he could relax a few minutes with the old books.

OSSIAN

Teddy spent the next few hours in ancient Rome—at least in his mind. By the time he was certain he had his Caesars straight, it was dark. Yawning, he stood up and stretched, and then he wandered over to the Whitcomb collection. He'd started reading a book from the collection last week. Which one was it? Oh, yes: *The Poems of Ossian*. The librarian had recommended it to him, saying it was Governor Whitcomb's favorite. Teddy took it back to his table and started reading. He found the book—supposedly the English translation of an epic cycle of Scottish poems from the early Dark Ages—to be fascinating. The main character, Ossian, was a blind bard who sang of the thrilling life and battles of Fingal, a Scotch warrior. Teddy was about halfway through when the librarian who'd recommended the book to him came over to tell him the library was closing.

Teddy was astonished. It couldn't be closing time yet. He wasn't finished with his book. "Like the book?" the librarian asked, seeing his shining eyes and faraway gaze.

Teddy nodded enthusiastically.

"Make a note of the place where you left off so you can find it again tomorrow," she advised before setting off to warn a few more students about closing time.

With a sigh, Teddy jotted down the page number in his writing tablet and closed the book. He piled his history texts into his rucksack . . . and paused, looking at *Ossian*. He was halfway through. He could finish it tonight and return it first thing in the morning, before his history exam. No one would notice it was gone. It wasn't like stealing. He would only be borrowing the book overnight. In a flash, Teddy thrust *Ossian* into his rucksack and quickly made his way out of the library. Behind him, a dark shadow that had lain sleeping peacefully among the tomes awakened and watched him go.

Teddy jogged swiftly across campus, heading back to his boardinghouse, eager to get back to *Ossian*. Around him, the night air seethed with unseen energy, and the gas lamps lining the street flickered as he passed underneath them. He nodded a greeting to his landlady, who was lighting the lamps on the porch to welcome her lodgers home. She nodded back at him and picked up her broom, ready to attack the brown oak leaves that had drifted onto the porch during the bright fall day. Teddy raced upstairs, threw his rucksack on the bed, and pulled out *The Poems of Ossian*. Lighting the oil lamp, he settled down in his favorite chair to read. And read. And read.

The wind picked up as the night progressed, hissing against the windows and rattling the panes. "*Ossssiiiiiiiiiiannnnnn,*" it moaned against the shutters of Teddy's second-floor room. The wick of Teddy's lantern flickered wildly, making the shadows dance around the room. Teddy, eyes glued to the pages of the book, barely noticed.

A tree branch thudded against the side of the house in time to a sepulchral chant hissed among the pines lining the yard. "Who . . . stole . . . *Ossian?*" In the boarding house, Teddy turned another page of the book.

Out on the front porch, the landlady swept the last of the autumn leaves from the steps and paused, shivering as she stared into the dark street. The wind tore through the branches of the large pine trees edging the property, hissing, "*Osssssian. Osssssian.*" Hastily, the landlady took her broom and scuttled inside, slamming shut the front door and locking it.

Along the empty street, a long shadow paced slowly beneath the glow of the streetlamps, though there was no person there to cast it . . . at least, no one visible. The footsteps echoed in the chilly evening air, and an unspoken voice whispered in the wind, "Who . . . stole . . . *Ossian?* Who . . . stole . . . *Ossian?*"

When the shadow reached the front of the apartment house, it stopped, and the wind rose around it, swirling brown oak leaves up into twin cyclones on either side of the walkway.

"*Ossssssian,*" the wind howled. "*Ossssian!*"

The invisible shadow-figure stared up at the lighted window above him. Through the pane, Teddy was clearly visible in his chair, eagerly turning the pages of the book. The shadow raised an arm and pointed toward the window. A pile of leaves upended itself and slammed against the side of the house in a *whoosh* of cold air. "*Ossssian,*" howled the wind. Still, Teddy didn't move.

Just then, two laughing students came striding down the road in high spirits, several bottles of whisky clutched in their arms. The shadow melted into the ground, and the leaves drifted silently to earth as the students came barreling up the walkway and let themselves in the front door with the spare key. Lights came on inside the house, and friendly voices echoed up and down the hallways. A few minutes later, the boarders, a dreamy-eyed Teddy among them, came to the dining room to eat supper. The shadow drifted quietly into the darkness under the pine trees, biding its time.

After dinner, the boarders made their way to their separate rooms, Teddy racing ahead of them all, eager to get back to his book. Slowly, the lights went out in each of the rooms, except the front room upstairs, where Teddy sat reading in his nightshirt, his nightcap askew over one eye, still mesmerized by *Ossian.*

It was nearly midnight when Teddy turned the final pages of *The Poems of Ossian* and shut the book with a satisfied sigh, his eyelids drooping. He thought about going back to his history books, but a moment later, he nodded off in the chair, *Ossian* still clutched to his chest.

As the big grandfather clock struck midnight in the hallway downstairs, the front door burst open, and hurricane-force winds blew colored leaves all around the entryway, bringing the chill of winter with them. A black shadow-figure, darker than the surrounding night, stepped inside. "*Ossssian,*" it hissed. "Who . . . stole . . . *Ossian?*"

Inside the downstairs rooms, the lodgers shivered and rolled deeper into their beds. But the shadow had no interest in them. It walked toward the stairs in a pit of darkness that sucked on the eye. "*Ossssian,*" it whispered as a shadow foot lifted to the first step. With each thud of a footfall came a word of the agitated chant: "Who, *thud* . . . stole, *thud* . . . *Ossian, thud?* Who, *thud* . . . stole, *thud* . . . *Ossian, thud?*"

At the top of the stairs, the shadow pointed to Teddy's door. blowing it open with a loud bang. Teddy woke with a start to see the silhouette of a black figure, all swirling energy and eyeball-sucking darkness, standing in the doorway. The wick of the oil lamp beside the chair flickered wildly in the strange airless breeze. The black figure strode toward the cowering student, looming taller and taller in the guttering light of the lamp. It's arm whipped out suddenly from the shadows surrounding it, and a bony finger pointed an inch from Teddy's nose. "Who . . . stole . . . . *Ossian?*" the shadow man hissed.

"I only borrowed it!" Teddy shrieked in terror.

Then, Teddy ducked under the skeletal arm of the shadow figure, jumped out of bed, and flung himself out the door, down the steps, and out of the house . . . *Ossian* still clutched to his chest.

Early the next morning, the librarian whose job it was to unlock the front door of the library found Teddy huddled on the doorstep with *The Poems of Ossian* gripped in trembling hands. "I borrowed it from the restricted collection," he gasped when he saw the librarian. "I'm sorry." Teddy thrust the book into the librarian's hands and ran away as if all the demons of hell were at his heels. Perhaps they were. Puzzled, the librarian stared after him for a moment before taking the book back into the library to be shelved.

In the shadows above the lintel, a dark figure smiled as the librarian slipped his favorite book back onto the shelf. "*Ossian,*" it murmured . . . and then vanished.

8

The Lady in Black

MORGAN-MONROE STATE FOREST

The lady was so happy . . . ecstatically happy. She had married the man she loved, and now she had a child, a perfect baby girl. There was nothing more she wanted. She went about her daily tasks with a song in her heart and a smile on her lips for everyone she met.

Perhaps she was too happy. Perhaps fate despised so great a joy when so many others were living in despair. Whatever the reason, it came as a body-blow when her husband, her beloved help-mate, died in a quarry accident in the third year of their marriage. The lady was devastated. Her young husband was laid to rest in Stepp Cemetery, and she visited his grave every day, carrying their small daughter with her.

Her daughter became everything to the young widow. She guarded the child carefully when she was a toddler and was extremely strict with the girl when she went to school. Homework was always done on time. All visits with friends were supervised. Only activities that were educational in nature were permitted. Church was attended every week.

The situation grew worse as the girl grew older. She was a beauty like her mother, and the boys flocked around her at school.

But her mother was jealous of their attention. When other girls went to the local soda shop or the moving pictures with their beaus, the lady made her daughter stay at home and study.

In her junior year, the daughter became obsessed with the prom. She wanted to go. She needed to go. Every other girl in her class was going; she would be ashamed to show her face in school if she didn't go. The teen spent the first six months of school begging her mother for this one treat, this one chance to be like all the other girls. Finally, she wore down her mother, who relented to her precious daughter going to the prom only if she went with the neighbor's son, a trustworthy boy who attended their church. The daughter made a face when she heard the condition, but she agreed. Anything to go to the prom!

Unbeknownst to the lady, this self-same boy had been secretly courting her lovely daughter for months. In the evening, when the daughter went up to her bedroom, ostensibly to study, she would creep down the tree outside her window and visit her secret beau. On the night her mother told her daughter she could go to the prom, the young couple boldly went to the soda shop and ordered ice cream sundaes, just like the other high school sweethearts. They even held hands under the table.

The daughter bought a wonderful sparkly silver dress to wear to the prom. The neighbor boy picked her up right on time and presented her with a perfect corsage. The lady gave him a long lecture on correct behavior and her high expectations. She even hinted that the neighbor boy might be welcome again in their home if he behaved himself and brought her daughter home by ten o'clock that night. He eagerly promised to have the daughter home by curfew, overjoyed at the possibility of being able to court her openly after the prom. The daughter and her date discussed it all the way to the high school, eagerly making plans for picnics and movie nights with their friends once the lady had sanctioned their courtship.

At home, the lady fussed around the house and watched the clock, worrying lest something happen to her daughter. Would some boy accost her? Would someone spike the punch? Would she stuff herself on sweets and fall ill? Surely not. The neighbor's boy was a trustworthy lad. He would take care of her daughter.

At the prom, the daughter and her beau danced and laughed and danced again. Around nine, he suggested they sneak off early and do some parking, like the other high school sweethearts. The daughter was ecstatic. She'd never been parking before! They went to the local lovers' lane by the cemetery, and as a light rain fell on the car, they held hands and made plans for their future. The boy even managed to sneak in a kiss or two before the girl coyly held him off and reminded him of his promise to her mother. Thus reminded of the strict old lady, the neighbor boy casually checked his watch and gasped in shock. It was fifteen minutes to ten! There was not a minute to spare if he wanted to get his girl home before curfew.

"We must go! We must hurry!" the daughter cried. "Mother will never allow us to date again if we miss curfew!"

Her beau gunned the engine and raced down the winding, narrow road, accelerating on every straightaway. He must get her home on time. He must. The car fishtailed on the slippery, rain-slicked roads, and the boy fought for control as they rounded a corner. The daughter gasped and then sighed with relief as the wheels caught some traction and the car straightened out. Abruptly, the car spun out of control, spinning once, twice. It slammed into a tree and shuddered to a halt. The boy smashed his head on the dashboard, dying on impact. The daughter flew through the shattered windshield, past the tree, and into the barbed wire fence in the nearby field. Her body was sliced into pieces by the cruel wire, and her head was lopped off at the neck.

Ten o'clock passed and then eleven o'clock with no sign of the daughter or her beau. Frantic with worry, the lady and her neighbors drove around town looking for their missing children. When they saw the lights of a police car ahead of them, the lady gave a cry of great fear, knowing instinctively that her daughter was dead. She flew out of the car, brushing past the police officers and falling to her knees beside her daughter's decapitated form, weeping bitterly while the neighbor couple clung together in agony, staring at the totaled car containing the body of their son.

The two young people were buried in their families' plots in Stepp Cemetery. Somehow, life went on for the neighbors and for the deceased young sweethearts' high school friends. But it stopped for the lady. Her hair turned silver-white overnight, and her face grew suddenly lined and gray. She made it through the burial—barely—and then collapsed. From then on, she dressed head-to-toe in black, ate infrequently, and rarely slept. She spent most nights sitting on a roughly carved tree stump in the cemetery, crying and talking to the graves of her lost husband and daughter.

Time passed, but the lady's sorrow did not. Grim-faced and silent, she went about her tasks during the day and returned, weeping, to the graveyard each night. Finally, the lady's terrible grief drove her insane, and she was put in a mental institution, where she died a few months later.

THE LADY IN BLACK

A month to the day after the lady's death, one of her daughter's high school friends and her beau went parking in the lover's lane near the cemetery. They kissed and cuddled in the front seat of the big old car, and the girl gave a laughing shriek when a thump rocked the vehicle, thinking her boyfriend was teasing her. Her shriek turned into a scream when she saw a glowing, dark figure loom menacingly beside the car. Staring in the window was a silver-haired woman dressed all in black. Around her neck she wore a tattered, blood-stained human head, which she raised with her gnarled hands. She glared a warning through the windshield of the car. The girl and boy both recognized the battered head as that of the woman's daughter, their dead friend from high school. The girl screamed and fainted as her boyfriend started the car with shaking hands and backed the car away from the glowing figure. He swung out onto the road with a hammering heart and squealing tires. Then, reminded of how the ghost's daughter had died, he slowed down as soon as the dark figure was out of sight and drove cautiously through the winding narrow road until he reached his girlfriend's home.

The courting couple was the first, but certainly not the last, to see the Lady in Black. Even after local high school students— fearing the wrath of the ghost—gave up on the cemetery as a lover's lane, the Lady in Black continued to appear to folks brave enough to visit Stepp Cemetery. To this day, she can be seen walking through the graveyard, her long, silver hair aglow against her black gown. And sometimes, she sits on the old stump-chair, weeping softly and talking to the tombs.

9

The Face

He toppled into love the moment he set eyes on the new transfer student in late August when classes started for the semester. She was an art major, and he was a poor medical student who didn't talk much about his family, on account of his father. His father had gone insane in traffic one day and tried to run over several pedestrians who were blocking the street. His father had been locked away in an asylum, and the family never mentioned him.

But his father was not on his mind the day he met Sheila. She was a lovely girl with masses of long, black hair and eyelashes so long they got tangled in her curls when she leaned over her desk. He had a withdrawn nature, though not by inclination. He'd learned the hard way that friends started acting funny when they learned about his insane father. So he'd stopped having friends. If anyone inquired about his family, he told them his father was dead rather than admit the truth. Now, he had to overcome his taciturn nature or risk losing Sheila to one of the other fellows who panted after her.

He studied her habits as closely as she studied her books, and soon he found a way to be close to her. She had a favorite spot in the library where she always studied between classes. He started studying in a cubicle nearby, and a couple of "chance" encounters between them turned into a conversation. Then, he volunteered to tutor her in one of her classes. From there, it was easy. Sheila toppled into love with him, too, almost as madly as he had fallen for her.

The new college sweethearts went everywhere together, hardly bearing to part for classes. He lived in a bubble of joy . . . until the Tuesday he saw her leaving her history class next to a good-looking fellow who lived in the same dorm. They were laughing together over something the professor had said in class, and a shaft of sheer jealousy pierced his gut. How dare she laugh with another man?

The boyfriend confronted his wayward girlfriend with her perceived trespass, and she stared at him incredulously. "You're crazy!" she said.

He winced, reminded of his father. That set him off. He started yelling at her, accusing her of all sorts of things, and she stalked off in a rage. He huddled in his dorm room, feeling miserable and vowing to forget her. But they made up over dinner, and things were fine for a while.

But one day the boyfriend saw her borrowing a pen from a handsome blond fellow at the library. That set him off again. The two young lovers hissed angry words at each other until the librarian kicked them out. Again, Sheila stalked off in a rage, as he shouted nasty things at her retreating back. Again, he huddled on the narrow bed in his dorm room, feeling miserable and vowing to forget her, until the black anger gave way to common sense. He called Sheila and apologized. She accepted his apology, and they agreed to get back together. In a flush of excited relief, he asked her to the dance on Friday, and she accepted.

THE FACE

The boyfriend's hands trembled with excitement as he packed his medical bag after class on Friday. He rushed back to the dorm, threw his bag on the desk, and dressed in his best. He picked Sheila up at her dorm room and escorted her to the dance. It was a wonderful night. Sheila had bought a new yellow dress—a lovely concoction with a swirling skirt and a little bit of a top. She looked stunning. The boyfriend's head whirled at the sight of her, and he could hardly keep his hands away from her. They danced, drank, and ate appetizers until Sheila called a laughing halt to the eating, saying she'd gained ten pounds in the last ten minutes. He'd laughed along with her and told her they would dance it off, which they did. They left early and walked hand-in-hand back to his dorm room for a nightcap.

When they reached the entrance to the dorm, Sheila veered off for a moment to speak with a red-haired fellow who was in one of her art classes, wanting to know about an assignment that was due the next day. The boyfriend stood impatiently just inside the door, frowning as the art student beamed at Sheila in the gorgeous, little yellow dress. When she smiled back at him, the red-haired art student looked stunned.

The inside of the boyfriend's skull throbbed from a sudden headache, brought on by too much alcohol combined with gut-gnawing jealousy. When Sheila rejoined him, he grabbed her hand roughly and hustled her upstairs to his room.

"Stop rushing! You're hurting my hand!" Sheila protested as he swept them both inside.

A quick glance told him that his roommate was out. Good. He rounded on Sheila and shouted, "You are hurting my heart! You flirt with every man you meet, you tramp!"

Sheila's face flushed scarlet with fury, and she shouted back at him, accusing him of flirting with the female medical students and of being so jealous she couldn't ask a seventy-year-old man for directions without setting him off. "You are crazy!" she shouted at him. "Stark raving mad!"

The boyfriend saw red. It rose around the edges of his eyesight, billowing like clouds. He groped through the red mists, and his hands found his medical bag. "Don't call me mad!" he said through gritted teeth, and his hands closed on a scalpel.

When the mists cleared from his eyes, Sheila lay dead at his feet, her throat cut from ear to ear. The whole room was covered with red gore, and her masses of black hair lay in a pool of streaming blood.

It had been a silent murder. Sheila hadn't believed her eyes until it was too late to scream . . . too late to do anything but die. The boyfriend had cut her windpipe with medical precision, though he didn't remember anything that happened after the red mist had obscured his eyesight.

His brain went into overdrive. Hide the body. Clean up the blood. Invent an alibi. But first . . . He stared at the face he loved so much. Dead now. Gone, out of his reach. The red mist rose a little in his mind as he knelt beside the body and slowly cut off her face. He wrapped the face carefully in plastic before putting it in his desk drawer. Then, he cleaned up the blood, tucked the body into a blanket, and stuck it under his bed until the middle of the night, when he carried it downstairs and hid it in the tunnel near the laundry room.

The next day, the boyfriend told his roommate that he and Sheila had broken up and she'd gone home in a snit without finishing her classes. He patted his desk drawer absently as he spoke. Once his roommate turned back to his books, he peered at the face inside. Yes, Sheila was still there.

The face seemed to draw him, just as Sheila's presence had once done. The boyfriend kept wandering over to the desk to peer inside several times an hour. His roommate sat studying on the other bed and didn't seem to notice his restlessness, which was just as well. He had to get a grip on himself, start studying for final exams.

Finally, the boyfriend went to the vending machine to buy a soda. When he got back, his roommate was leaning out the open window, looking ill.

"I think I have the flu," the roommate said when he came in.

"Want me to take a look?" the boyfriend offered, reaching for his medical bag.

His roommate turned white and barked, "No! Thank you! Don't bother. I'll just pick up something at the pharmacy." At that, he hurried out of the room, practically running.

The boyfriend settled down at the desk, peered in the drawer at the face, and then began work on a paper he had due next week. He could feel Sheila's presence beside him. She was helping him with his homework, he thought happily. Downstairs, his roommate was on the phone with the police.

The boyfriend went ballistic when the police came with a warrant to arrest him. They manhandled him out of his chair and over to the door. A grim-faced officer took a look in the desk drawer and then turned around and vomited on the floor. The boyfriend roared at the sacrilege. No other man was allowed to look at his girlfriend's face! It belonged to him! How dare they? He screamed all the way down the stairs and out of the dorm.

Students peered out their doors as he fought the hold of the policemen, lunging this way and that in his fury.

When the boyfriend realized they were leaving Sheila's face behind in the dorm where any man might see it, he panicked. "Don't take her away from me," he pleaded with the officer as the man bundled him into the car. "I want her with me always! Don't take her away!" He reached his handcuffed arms toward the man, who backed away and slammed the door on him. The boyfriend lay back against the seat and sobbed in misery: "Sheila . . . Sheila . . . Sheila . . ."

His family had him transferred to the asylum where his father was kept locked up in a padded room. Every day, his enraged father tried to kill his attendants, while the bereft boyfriend wept and stared out the window. The boyfriend kept seeing Sheila's lovely face in the branches of a nearby tree. The face seemed to sway in rhythm to his father's fists pounding on the walls in the room next door to his son.

And in the dorm, the amorphous ghost of a young girl in a bloodstained yellow dress floats along the hallways, looking for her face.

Counterfeit

In hindsight, I probably should have questioned my new employees more thoroughly before hiring them to excavate trenches through the tight crawlspaces in my newly purchased cave. But I was eager to create an easy path that would allow visitors to walk through the amazing caverns without the need to crawl through the narrower passages, and the local contractors didn't favor backbreaking work in a dark cave. So I welcomed the three men who came in answer to my sign and hired them at once, even though they requested nighttime working hours. It was a strange request. When I questioned them about it, they gave me evasive answers, which made me rather suspicious. Still, I needed the work done, and no one else had applied for the job, so I consented to their strange stipulation.

I didn't see my new employees at all the first week, except on Friday morning when they came for their money. However, an expedition to the cave showed me that the excavation was moving forward as planned. They were working hard, and already some of the tighter passages had been enlarged enough to walk through. Very good.

COUNTERFEIT

A few more weeks passed in this manner. Then, one of my tour guides popped in to see me after his shift. He'd gone exploring in some of the back passages that were closed to visitors and found a large crate in an otherwise empty cavern room.

"A crate?" I exclaimed. "What in tarnation is a crate doing in a back room of my cave?"

"Sir, I don't know," the man replied. "I thought I should report it."

"Yes, yes. Well done," I said. "I will look into it at once." I thanked the man and sent him home to his dinner.

As soon as time permitted, I took a lantern and descended along the passages until I reached the room in question. In the flickering lantern light, I saw a large crate standing on the floor of the cavern. What the devil? I inspected the box, which had no writing on it. I opened the lid. The glow of the lantern fell upon a strange contraption of some sort. I poked at it cautiously. It looked almost like a printing press. Then, I saw the plates inside the machine and realized I was looking at an engraving of US currency.

"Counterfeiters!" I gasped aloud.

Why had counterfeiters hidden their printing press in my cave? When? Who? Could it be one of the tour guides? No, I knew all of them well. Were some of the locals using my cave for their illegal activity? How had they gotten in? Then, I remembered my new hires, the men who were excavating the tunnels, the men who only worked at night. Now, I knew the reason for their strange hours.

I had to report it at once. If I let it go on without turning them in, I ran the risk of being implicated in their counterfeiting operation. I saddled up my horse and rode into Leavenworth to speak to the sheriff. He was skeptical at first. Rural Indiana didn't seem a likely place to run a counterfeiting operation. But a trip to the cave convinced him, and we made plans to ambush the counterfeiters the very next morning—which was Friday— when I went to the entrance of the cave to give them their pay.

Dawn was coloring the sky when I strolled toward the cave with the counterfeiters' pay envelopes in the pocket of my jacket. The sheriff and his men were hidden near the entrance to the cavern, just as we'd planned. I could see them, but the counterfeiters emerging from the dark cavern would not, until it was too late. I stood waiting in the chilly morning air, keeping myself calm by reciting the times tables in my head. Suddenly, I heard voices echoing from the cave entrance. Then, lights appeared in the darkness like bobbing stars. A moment later, three men emerged, grubby from a night's hard work and blinking in the growing light of day. The deputies came running from either side of the entrance, shouting to the criminals to stop and put up their hands. The deputies managed to get the jump on two of the men, but the third, walking a couple of steps behind his friends, whirled and ran back into the cave.

"After him!" shouted the sheriff, gesturing to several of his deputies to light torches while others secured the two prisoners. I watched them follow the counterfeiter into the cave and waited anxiously for their return.

A long time later the sheriff and his men stumbled from the entrance, empty-handed. "We paused at intervals to listen for the sound of footsteps," the sheriff told me. "The torches cast so many shadows that it was hard to see into every cranny of every room. That place is a maze! By the time we reached the Mountain Room, the footsteps had died away. We figured he'd doubled back to the entrance, but nobody saw him on the way out. The darned fellow's got clean away."

"He won't get far without food or water," I told the sheriff. "He must come out sooner or later."

"True," he conceded. So he set a guard upon the entrance and took his remaining prisoners back to Leavenworth.

Days passed, and then weeks. By the end of the third week, the sheriff decided that the counterfeiter must have gotten lost in one of the uncharted tunnels and perished.

"Or perhaps he caused an avalanche in the Mountain Room," a deputy suggested. "He could have been buried underneath all that rubble, and how would we know?"

That being entirely possible, the watch was abandoned, and things returned to normal. Tourists came to visit the cavern. I got on with my work. And the remaining counterfeiters were taken before a judge and sentenced accordingly.

Still, I shouldn't have been surprised when my tour guides began reporting that the shadowy figure of a man sometimes appeared in the Mountain Room, wandering around the perimeter of the space as if searching for a way out. He wasn't one of the tourists, and he vanished whenever a guide stepped toward him. Sometimes, cave visitors reported that they felt someone was following them along the excavated passages, but when they turned around, no one was there. I was afraid stories about the ghost would discourage the tourist trade, but that never happened. In fact, I think some people visited the cave just to hear about the counterfeiter's ghost.

I, myself, never saw the ghost, but I heard it once, a few years after the counterfeiter disappeared in the cave. I was standing in the Mountain Room after hours, inspecting a repair, when

I heard a man's voice shouting for help deep inside the cavern. Technically, I was the only person inside the cave at that time of day. Still, I figured one of the tour guides might be doing some exploring and gotten himself turned around. I followed the voice for a few minutes, determined to rescue whoever was trapped in the cave. As I walked through the passageways, the voice changed direction several times, jumping from spot to spot faster than a human could run. I suddenly realized that I did not hear any footsteps save my own. That gave me goose bumps

I followed the voice around in a complete circle, finally returning to the Mountain Room, where I'd first heard the man calling. By then, the strangeness of the situation was getting to me. The hairs on my arms stood on end, and icy shudders crept across my skin.

"It must be the counterfeiter's ghost," I said aloud. I was answered instantly.

"Help me," the voice wailed suddenly, right in front of me.

I froze in fear. The sound came from the rubble at the foot of the mountain. I raised my lantern, but no one appeared in the flickering light.

Trembling, I said: "Rest in peace, my friend. Rest in peace."

Silence fell over the room, and suddenly my fear went away. The ghost was gone.

It was hard to go into the cave the next day, but I did it. I had to. I owned the place. To my relief, no shadow lurked in the Mountain Room, and the only voices I heard were those of tourists.

"Tell me about the ghost," one little boy demanded excitedly, tugging on the hand of the tour guide.

I didn't stay to listen. I had work to do.

Train Wreck

HAMMOND

Many of my fellow engineers did not like riding the Michigan City line, but I had no idea why. Employees were discouraged from discussing the matter, and we newbies on the line were left to wonder.

I'd been riding the rails for about six months when I was switched to the night shift. I didn't mind. My wife had passed away a few years back from cancer, and we didn't have any children, so things were pretty lonely around my place. I spent more time at the rail yards than I did at home.

I noticed right away that the atmosphere along the Michigan City track was very different at night. Now, I'm a lifetime railroader. I've driven many a train through the darkest of nights and the brightest of dawns, and most railroad tracks felt the same no matter what time it was. But not this one. Once we were through Gary, the night grew darker, and the headlights didn't illuminate the track so well. The air along the line felt chilled and clammy, even when the temperature was in the nineties. And once when I passed the turn-off for the Michigan Central tracks, I heard a man's voice say in a choked wail, "I was dozing." This creeped me out something terrible, because at the time I was alone in the cab. I knew then that the track was haunted. It had to be. Either that, or I was going mad—an increasingly likely option.

Two nights later, I got a call on the radio ordering me to pull the train off onto the Michigan Central tracks leading into Hammond to allow an express train to pass us. I don't mind admitting I got the willies when I heard that. It was the very same spot in which I'd heard the phantom voice a couple of nights earlier. But orders were orders, so I slowed the train and turned off. Once we were clear of the other line, I stopped the train, knowing I'd have to reverse myself once the express train was through.

Suddenly, I heard a hiss of steam and the chug and roar of a train from the other line. I turned to look back toward the Michigan City line, puzzled. Why was I hearing an old-time steam train coming down the line at full throttle? I was expecting a passenger express, not some old-fashioned holiday excursion special. I saw headlights coming down the track and wondered why in the world an excursion train was running at 4:00 a.m.? And why hadn't they radioed to tell me that two trains would pass us instead of just one? Then, I saw a red flare burst into life, followed by another, and I heard a man shouting in alarm.

"What's going on?" I exclaimed, leaping out of the cab.

That's when all hell broke loose on the line, literally. First, I heard a crash . . . then a roar . . . and then *thud, thud, thud, thud, thud*—like a million bricks crashing onto a tin roof. There was a moment of terrible silence. And then the world exploded in a mind-jarring blur of white light and flames that I could see and hear but not feel. A moment later, the world around me went pitch-black, although the sound of the inferno continued. People screamed in pain and terror. Moans and sobs split the night air. I heard the sound of metal and wood crashing down all around me, but all I could feel was the cool night breeze on my skin. I rubbed my eyes, dazzled by the light I'd seen. Spots appeared with every blink, and I didn't know if I were seeing ghosts or just the dazzle spots you get after looking at a bright lamp. Footsteps raced past me, and I heard a man's voice desperately calling for help.

"My wife," he shouted, his voice breaking with fear. "Where's my wife?"

Toward the back of my own train, I heard a wordless moaning, as if someone were dying in torment. I shone my flashlight in that direction, but the tracks were empty.

The sounds ceased as abruptly as they started, and I heard the express train coming down the Michigan City tracks. A pair of headlights lit up the empty expanse of rails. I let out my breath, not realizing until then that I'd been holding it. Then, I bolted for the cab. Behind my train, the express roared past the turn-off. A moment later, the radio sounded to let me know the line was clear and I could resume my journey.

I backed slowly out onto the Michigan City line, shuddering inside as I realized my train was moving over the same tracks where the fiery inferno had taken place just a few moments—or was it a lifetime?—ago. As I switched out of reverse and headed back down the track, I decided it was best not to mention the strange incident to my supervisor. He would think I was crazy . . . or worse, fire me for lying.

I did search out one of the old-timers and stood him to a drink at the local bar in exchange for information regarding the pull-off toward Hammond. He nodded wisely when I mentioned seeing a light on the tracks and hearing an explosion. "That would be the circus train," he said. "Bad wreck back in nineteen-eighteen."

I pressed for more information, but that was all he would tell me. So I went to the library and looked it up. The wreck happened on June 22, 1918, at 3:57 a.m. The Hagenbeck-Wallace Circus train—twenty-five cars containing 225 circus performers—was traveling overnight from Michigan City to Hammond. Just after the Colfax Street crossing, the brakeman in the caboose spotted a hotbox on one of the cars ahead. The engineer slowed the train at once, knowing a minor repair was needed that would probably halt the train for about fifteen minutes. By the time the train rumbled to a stop, the first half had turned onto the Michigan Central tracks, leaving five passenger cars and the caboose at a standstill on the main line. Johnson, the engineer of the circus train, knew that Signal 2581 had gone red behind them, telling any trains on the Michigan City line to stop, so the circus train was safe for the moment and could make the necessary repair.

Hard on the heels of the circus train came Engine 8485, pulling an empty troop train. The steam train was on full-throttle and didn't even slow down when it reached the Ivanhoe station or the Colfax crossing. The engineer driving the train was sick that night and had fallen asleep at the controls.

I paused in my reading, goose bumps rising all over my arms and legs. Asleep at the controls? I remembered the man's voice wailing in my ear as I passed the Michigan Central line several days ago: "I was dozing." I shuddered all over and went back to the newspaper account of the fatal train wreck.

TRAIN WRECK

The brakeman on the caboose was the first one to see the oncoming troop train. Thinking fast, he lit several flares and waved them at the approaching engine. When it didn't slow, he threw a flare directly at the cab. The flare was still sparking on the engine when the troop train crashed at full speed into the caboose and kept going, telescoping the five wooden passenger cars that were standing helpless on the Michigan City line. Within moments, the passenger cars were on fire, and when the fire hit the gasoline-fueled lamps, the wrecked turned into a fiery inferno. When the fire died down around mid-morning of the next day, most of the dead passengers were found in a pile just in front of Engine 8485.

Only twenty-four of the bodies found at the wreck were identifiable. Most of the others were charred and mangled beyond recognition. The general manager of the circus ran a hasty tabulation of scattered employees and said it was probable that eighty-five persons had been killed. Most were buried in a mass grave in "Showmen's League Rest," a portion of Woodlawn cemetery owned by the Showmen's League of America.

The list of the dead included bareback riders, animal trainers, the strong man, a famous equestrienne, a family of elephant trainers, and a husband–wife aerialist team.

The circus community rallied around the beleaguered show, lending acts and supplies. Two days after the crash, the Hagenbeck-Wallace circus was back in business, missing only two of its scheduled shows that season.

I turned away from my reading, saddened by the terrible tragedy that had happened so many years ago and that had been reenacted so graphically out on the tracks. I hoped that someday the memory of the terrible tragedy would fade and the circus performers and their families could rest in peace. In the meantime, I would ask my supervisor if I could switch to the day shift. I'd had enough tragedy to last me for a good long while.

Granny's Revenge

PERU

Sally was elated when the will was read and she learned that her late grandfather had left her and her two sisters an old house just outside Peru. She'd had no idea that her stingy old grandfather owned any property. He'd lived in a boardinghouse for the last twenty years, the whole of Sally's life. He'd moved into the room after the death of his wife and had groused about the expense ever after. Whenever the sisters came to visit their grandfather, the stingy old curmudgeon had cursed at them because they bore the bloodline of his late wife, whom he hated with a passion. He accused them of courting him for his money, which was laughable, considering the state of destitution he lived in. But the sisters had promised their parents—who'd died in a fever epidemic in 1887—that they would look after the old man, so they had visited him faithfully. Sally had hated every minute of those tortuous afternoons, though. Now, it turned out that Grandfather had had plenty of money all along and a house to boot.

"From penury to plenty in one hour," said her sister Maude when they left the attorney's office.

"Why did he live in poverty?" asked Earline, the youngest sister.

"Who knows?" Sally said with an expressive wave of her hand. "He was a crackpot."

The three sisters decided to move into their new house immediately. They'd been renting a two-room cottage, which was far too small for the three of them. While Sally gave notice to their landlord, her sisters packed their belongings into a hired wagon. As they drove over the rain-rutted roads toward Peru, they rejoiced in their good fortune.

"I wonder why grandfather never mentioned the house," Earline said nervously as they drove along the narrow lane leading toward town. "You'd think he'd have lived in it all these years. Do you think something is wrong?"

"I think the only thing wrong was grandfather," said Maude briskly. "He was crazy in the head, Earline. Imagine living in a boardinghouse when he owned property in Peru!"

"That's what I mean," said Earline. "There must be something wrong with the house. Grandfather wouldn't have paid a penny to live in a boardinghouse unless he had to."

"Grandfather was strange, Earline," Sally said crisply, urging the horse into a trot. "That's your answer."

Sally was eager to get to Peru to claim their inheritance. They'd been poor all their lives. Suddenly, they had property and a house of their own. Who cared why the strange old man had abandoned it? She touched the huge, iron door key in the pocket of her shabby overcoat. It was the key to their new life.

Following the directions the attorney had given them when he'd dropped off the key, Sally made her way across town and eventually turned down a narrow road leading to their new home. Twilight was falling when they reached the gate, and Sally pulled the horse to a halt so they could inspect the property.

A silence fell over the sisters as they looked at the swayback old house with its sagging roof, cracked window panes, and ivy-covered walls. Several floorboards were missing from the front porch, and the steps were so warped they seemed to lead toward the side yard instead of the front door. Dark, shadowy woods crept to the very edge of the property, and shadows skulked in the overgrown garden. Earline gulped audibly, and Sally bit back an exclamation of horror. No comfortable homecoming awaited them here. The fireplaces were probably blocked, and she wouldn't be surprised if squirrels had colonized the attic. Still, it belonged to them with no debts attached to it . . . for whatever it was worth.

"Well, it's ours," Maude said at last, unconsciously echoing Sally's thoughts. "Come on. There's a barn out back. Let's put the horse in there and get the wagon unloaded before it's too dark to see." Maude was the practical sister.

The sisters stabled the horse in the run-down old barn and then carried the most essential bundles toward the house. It looked just as downtrodden and spooky from the back as it did from the front.

Suddenly, Earline gasped and grabbed Sally's arm. "What's that?" she shrieked, gesturing toward a second-story window as Sally dropped her parcels all over the ground.

"What's what?" snapped Sally as she bent to retrieve her boxes.

"I saw something in the window," cried Earline.

"Nonsense," said Maude and Sally almost simultaneously.

"I was staring at the house the whole time," Maude continued. "There's nothing there."

The three sisters studied the darkened building for a long moment. Nothing moved in the shadows. There wasn't even a stray breeze to stir the riot of ivy that covered everything.

It would be very easy to imagine a dark figure staring out one of those empty dark rectangles, Sally thought nervously. The old house seemed to loom over them with an air of doom that made her flesh creep.

"Nonsense!" Maude said again, breaking the silence. "Let's go in." She marched up the weed-entangled walkway and pushed at the back door.

"You need the key," Sally called to Maude.

But Maude didn't need the key. With a long, low moan, the door swung open. Earline shrieked again at the sound. Sally wanted to shake her youngest sister. Earline was making them nervous on purpose, she was sure. Honestly. That girl had never grown up. Sally marched up to the door and followed Maude inside.

She stepped into a shadowy room that might have been the kitchen. It was impossible to see anything through the ivy-strewn window, especially now that twilight had fallen over the garden outside. Maude fumbled in her topmost box and pulled out a lantern. After a few fumbles, she lit it and held it up. The sisters gazed around the ramshackle kitchen. The massive fireplace was a gaping black mouth at the far end of the room. The pump in the sink was red with rust. The table in the middle of the room sagged as badly in the center as the roof did.

"There are six inches of dust in here," Maude said with a sneeze. "And rats have made a nest in that kettle." She gestured to an overturned black pot lying in the fireplace. "We don't dare make a fire until we've checked to see if the chimney is blocked."

Maude strode forward and dumped her packages on the sagging table. Sally left hers by the pump, and Earline crept cautiously through the back door to lay her parcels near the

GRANNY'S REVENGE

fireplace. Her teeth were chattering as she eyed the door-shaped black gap in the wall beside the fireplace.

"Should we explore now or wait until morning?" Earline asked.

"I, for one, do not want to sleep in the kitchen," Sally said firmly. "Let's explore."

As Sally walked toward the door, the air around her grew frigid and crisp, as if she'd stepped outside on a cold winter morning. Her breath iced up in the lantern light, and for a moment, she thought she heard a woman's voice whisper "ahhhhhhh" somewhere inside her skull.

"What was that?" Sally asked sharply, whirling to look around.

Maude, busy wiping dust off the table, looked around irritably. "Now who's being a fraidy-cat?" she asked. "Come on!"

Maude walked into the hall carrying the oval yellow light of the lantern with her. The shadows she left behind were too dark for comfort. Sally and Earline scuttled after her. The sisters passed through room after room. What furniture there was had splintered or rotted away. An old piano was missing most of its keys. A floor-to-ceiling bookcase was filled with mildewed volumes. Dusty cobwebs were so thick they floated down from the ceiling like wedding veils and stirred ominously in the breeze of the sisters' passing.

Maude creaked her way upstairs, leaving footprints on every step. Sally was right on her heels, with Earline whimpering at the rear. When a rat scuttled across the landing, Earline screamed.

"Hush!" Maude and Sally said together. They didn't like making noise in that creepy old house. Sally was afraid they might awaken something that was best left asleep.

The three sisters turned the corner into the upper hall and looked into several old bedrooms. The largest contained a massive canopy bed with the canopy closed. There was so much dust on the canopy that it was impossible to tell what color it was. The sisters surveyed it in the flickering lantern light.

"I don't think so," Maude said slowly into the silence.

The air in the room was even colder than it had been in the kitchen, and Sally could almost picture a malevolent figure crouched behind that curtain.

"I think we should sleep in another room," Sally said firmly, pushing Earline back into the dusty, cobweb-strewn hallway.

In the end, the sisters retreated to the front bedroom, the only one with a window clear of ivy. The rising moon lit the dusty floor as they carried their bedding inside. There was a narrow bed in the corner, but it had been colonized by mice, and none of the sisters chose to sleep in it. They settled on the floor under their blankets and prepared to spend their first night in their new home.

It was after midnight when Sally woke suddenly, sure someone had called her name. She looked around the room, still bright with moonlight. Earline was curled up under the window, asleep with the blanket pulled up to her eyeballs as if to protect herself from evil spirits. But Maude's place was empty. Her blanket was strewn across the floor, and there was a dust-free spot where her body had lain. That was all.

"Maudie?" Sally called softly, trying not to waken Earline. "Where are you?"

Sally got up and picked up the lantern. Maybe Maude had gone to the privy? There was a broken-down old outhouse near the barn. She lit the lantern and stepped into the hallway to look out the window at the end, which faced the back yard and the barn.

"Maudie?" she called as she walked past the gaping black holes that were the doorways to the other bedrooms. The air around her grew colder as she neared the door to the main bedroom. Sally refused to look in at the canopied monstrosity inside. Surely, Maude wouldn't go in there? She glanced out the back window into the moonlit yard. It was empty.

Sally's neck pricked suddenly, and every hair on her body rose up in terror. There was something behind her. She could feel it's presence on her skin. She whirled around, lantern raised in defense, and saw a glowing woman with a crushed face and a curved blade half-embedded in her skull hovering in the air a foot behind her. She held a long, sharp scythe in her translucent hands.

"Child of my husband's get! How dare you come to this place where I was murdered?" the phantom screamed, raising the scythe.

Sally gasped in shock. She recognized the figure at once from an old photograph. It was her old granny.

Sally did not have time to ponder this revelation, for just then Granny swung the scythe straight at her head, meaning to decapitate her living granddaughter. Sally screamed and dodged into the first doorway she could find, the lantern falling to the floor of the hallway behind her. She rushed into the master bedroom and fell over something warm and sticky and foul. In the wildly flickering light of the fallen lantern, Sally saw the bloody body of her sister Maude, which had been sliced in half from head to toe.

Sally rolled through a warm puddle of gore, dodging the flailing scythe blade and somehow managing to get to her feet. She ran around the massive bed, the ghost on her heels, cursing and swinging. Sally leapt through the curtains into pitch darkness, rolled across a bony figure—it felt like a skeleton—and barreled through the other side, wrapped in rotting, dusty curtains. The phantom granny followed her, screeching and swinging the scythe.

Earline came running into the master bedroom, shouting for her sisters. She took one look at the glowing figure of her dead granny, the remains of the skeleton on the bed, the two halves of her eldest sister on the floor, and the curtain wrapped monstrosity that was Sally stumbling toward her and ran screaming down the hall. There was a sudden thumping sound, and the scream stopped abruptly. Sally ripped off the curtain at last and threw it on the floor, where it covered the gruesome remains of her sister Maude. She ran out into the hallway and saw the body of her baby sister at the bottom of the stairs. Earline's head was cocked at a strange angle; she was obviously dead of a broken neck.

"Dear God in Heaven!" Sally screamed. Then she whirled around as the phantom of her grandmother floated out of the master bedroom, scythe in hand.

"Granny, why are you killing us?" Sally shouted, her body shaking from head to toe.

"Your grandfather killed me for my money!" Granny shouted back, her crushed face twisted in rage. "As I coughed out the last of my life on that bed, I swore I would eradicate his line forever from this earth. He escaped my wrath, but you will not!"

The phantom scythe blade embedded in her skull seemed to catch fire as Granny's ghost swooped toward Sally.

Sally raced into the front bedroom and flung herself out the window, glass shattering all over the place as she fell down and down. As Sally bounced onto the roof of the front porch, she stared up at the phantom of her grandmother, who came right through the window after her granddaughter, scythe held in front of her like a sword. Sally rolled off the roof and fell into a briar bush. She pulled herself out of the brambles, barely noticing them rip her clothing to shreds as she ran toward the lane. She'd read somewhere that ghosts were tied to the place where they'd died. If she could just reach the edge of the property, she would be safe.

Sally felt the swish of the scythe blade cut off part of her long hair. She kept running, not looking back. The lane was right in front of her. Then a massive pain bit through her neck, and for one terrible instant she knew the scythe had caught her as she ran. Then, the world disappeared, and Sally's head flew off her body and rolled away into the shrubbery. The ghost of Granny shouted in triumph as she hovered above the slumped figure of her dead granddaughter. Her revenge was complete.

Part Two
Powers of Darkness and Light

13

Dog Face Bridge

SAN PIERRE

When my friend Diane suggested that we go to Dog Face Bridge to celebrate Halloween, I thought it was a great idea. I'd heard stories about the haunted bridge all my life, but I'd never visited it. So I called my girlfriend, Lisa, and Diane called her boyfriend, Cliff, and the four of us drove out to the bridge together at dusk to watch the sun go down and wait for something spooky to happen.

We decided Diane should drive her car, since she had a lead foot and was always getting speeding tickets. As I said to Lisa, when you are investigating the supernatural, you want someone fast in the driver's seat in case you need to make a quick getaway! Diane sat with Cliff in the front, and Lisa and I snuggled in the back as we drove and drove and drove through the darkening countryside. This place truly was in the middle of nowhere! To take our minds off the long drive, Diane related the history of the haunting as she'd heard it in school.

Sometime around 1950, a newly married couple was leaving San Pierre on their honeymoon trip. They were driving down Route 1100 West, laughing and chattering excitedly about their new life together as they drove over the first bridge and headed along the narrow road toward the second. The husband had just steered the car onto the second bridge when a dog came trotting toward them from the far end. The brand new husband swore and swerved to miss the creature, but the car skidded, knocking the dog off the bridge and plunging after it into the water below. The dog and the couple died instantly. Gruesomely, the heads of both the dog and the bride were severed from their bodies during the accident. The woman's head was found in the wreckage of the car near her dead husband, but her body was missing. The dog's body was found lying half-in and half-out of the water, but its head was missing.

Shocked and saddened by the tragedy, the town determined the road was too dangerous and closed off the bridges. And that was the end of the story . . . until rumors sprang up from the farmers and other townsfolk living near the sealed-up bridges. They talked of a bright light that appeared on the road and came swiftly toward the first bridge before disappearing abruptly. Rumors also spread of a phantom dog barking, and of a grotesque monster with the body of a woman and the head of a dog that nightly roamed the path between the two bridges. It was said that if the dog-woman caught a person walking on the old road, she would chase after them, barking shrilly. If her cold hands and sharp dog teeth caught the trespasser before he or she reached the first bridge, the victim's body would be wrenched apart and eaten, the tattered remains cast into the river where the dog and the couple had lost their lives. But if they reached the first bridge in time, the monster would turn away, to lie in wait for its next victim.

As Diane finished her gruesome tale, Lisa shivered in my arms and squealed: "Oh, my gosh! We should turn around. We're gonna die!"

"We're not going to die," I reassured her. "I'll protect you."

I was bluffing, of course. If the dog-woman existed, there was no way I would be able to save anyone from its malice, except maybe by running really, really fast. But Lisa liked my swagger, and she cuddled closer as we turned onto the old road leading toward the two bridges. It was a narrow road full of potholes, and Lisa grew more and more nervous as we drove into the darkening twilight. Diane flipped on the headlights, and Lisa screamed shrilly, pointing at a light shining ahead of us.

"It's the ghost light!" she cried, grabbing my arm so tightly she nearly cut off the circulation to my hand.

"It's just a reflector off the bridge," Cliff said calmly from his forward vantage point. "Relax, Lisa."

But Lisa was trembling so hard I knew we'd have trouble getting her out of the car. Diane, meantime, was doing a very tight K turn so that the car was aimed back down the road, in case we needed to make a quick getaway.

As soon as Diane turned off the engine, Cliff bolted out of the car with his flashlight and headed, whooping, toward the bridge. So much for secrecy. As I had predicted, Lisa went mulish and refused to leave the car. Finally, Diane handed her the car keys and made her get into the driver's seat.

"You be our getaway driver," Diane said to Lisa.

Relieved, Lisa nodded. I gave her a reassuring kiss and then followed the others.

I paused for a second at the road's dead end to stare at the bridge, standing just in front of the barrier blocking cars from crossing. I'd pictured a modern kind of bridge with guardrails, but it was one of those really old steel-structured bridges. Looking at it made goose bumps creep along my arms, and I started looking for a stick or something to defend myself with, just in case ol' dog-head showed up. I was leaning down to pick up a thick walking stick when I heard something heavy walking in the bushes about a foot away. It sounded heavy, as if it were a big animal or a tall person. (*Or both at once?* whispered a tiny voice in the back of my brain.) My pulse throbbed with fear, and I froze in my bent-over position. At once, the rustling ceased and the woods around me grew very quiet.

Then, a shout came from the bridge, breaking the spell of silence. "Come on, Gary! What are you waiting for?" It was Cliff, the enthusiast.

"I'm coming," I called back, grabbing up the stick and hurrying behind the barrier. Around me the wind picked up, making a sound like the ocean surf in the trees above. I could dimly see Diane and Cliff huddled together at the rusted railing, shining their flashlights in the water, but darkness was almost upon us, and I knew a few minutes more would turn them into dark figures, black on black. I dug out my own flashlight and turned it on, shining it cautiously down the length of the old bridge, looking for booby traps. I could see holes in the old road that crossed the rickety bridge, and as I looked, several small stones, loosened by the feet of my friends, fell down into one of the holes and splashed into the water below. I made a mental note of the position of the holes, having no desire to follow the rocks into the drink.

As I stepped onto the crumbly old bridge, I heard the sound of a dog barking way off in the distance. I froze, and the bridge seemed to rumble below my feet, like the growl of a big dog, although that might have been the wind, which was blowing up a gale overhead.

"What was that? Did you hear that?" Diane asked excitedly, staring down into the dark water.

"Just shut up and listen," Cliff replied with equal excitement.

For a moment I thought the bridge was going to collapse. It groaned and creaked in the wind as I made my way toward my friends, carefully avoiding the holes.

Cliff had spotted something to his right, all covered in weeds and leaves. He shone his flashlight on the object and gave a shout. "Look it's a tire! It's from the accident."

"It's not from the accident," I said, inching past another hole to reach the railing beside him. "The couple was killed on the second bridge, not the first one."

I gripped the railing and could feel the bridge trembling slightly beneath my hand, like a frightened puppy. It made me want to comfort it somehow, a ridiculous thought.

"Come on," said Diane. "The second bridge is down the path."

She loped across the bridge, flashlight darting here and there, illuminating rusted girders, a dark patch of water through a hole in the boards, a red-leaf bush growing beside the rail, and a man's shoe lying on the far side of the bridge. Cliff and I followed in her wake, catching up with her when the path narrowed and she was forced to slow down.

It was at this juncture that the whole expedition became surreal to me. The woods seemed to close in on us. The wind howled, and the trees rustled and shook, but the three of us seemed to be wrapped in a bubble of traveling silence. Every time I glanced into the dark trees on either side of us, I thought I saw pinpricks of light, like the reflection of light in a dog's eyes . . . a very tall dog. The size of a human? I shuddered. Diane was chattering enthusiastically to Cliff as we walked, but none of her words were registering in my ears. All I could hear was the roar of the wind. All I could feel was the strange bubble of silence around us.

That's when the barking began. It started on our right side, then switched with unnatural speed to the left, then to the right again. Diane shrieked and clutched at Cliff, almost banging him in the eye with her flashlight. I turned my flashlight this way and that, trying to follow the sound.

"Gary, let's get out of here!" shouted Cliff.

I agreed wholeheartedly and turned around . . . and saw the glowing figure of the dog-headed woman standing directly behind me! That's the terrible thing about phantoms; they don't follow normal rules.

The barking sound increased, now on both sides of the path, as if twenty dogs were closing in on our position. But the apparition in front of me was silent, as if she . . . it . . . were trapped in the bubble with us. It was tall, and the woman's body was clothed in a pretty floral traveling dress, circa 1950. The floral gown somehow made the dog's head rising from her neck seem even more grotesque, and the eyes in the dog's head glowed red.

I reeled back against Cliff and Diane, who whirled around to see what was wrong. Diane screamed, Cliff shouted, and I gave a sudden wild roar, bent over, and ran right at the monster, my head and shoulder tensed for impact. I plowed into the creature like a linebacker taking down an opponent, and for a moment my body was filled with a heart-stopping coldness. I caught strange visions from two perspectives: A looming car bore down on a small dog at the same instant the woman looked through

DOG FACE BRIDGE

the windshield and saw the same dog. Then, I was through and shouting to my friends to run. Run!

I heard Cliff dodging the phantom on the right side of the path and Diane crashing around it on the left. Light from the dog-headed woman glowed all around us, illuminating the trees eerily from underneath, highlighting the bottoms of the leaves that were still whipping in the wind. I ran for my life, faster than I'd ever gone before, the air puffing out of me like a bellows. I thought my heart would burst from the strain as I pounded down the path, Cliff and Diane right behind me. The glow followed behind them, lighting the trail in front of us and urging us on. The barking of the dogs simultaneously preceded us and roared at us from behind. I spotted the first bridge ahead and put on a burst of speed I normally did not possess. But adrenaline will do that for a fellow, and the adrenaline was sure pumping now. I was across the bridge in a heartbeat, Cliff and Diane still right behind me. As we dodged around the barrier, I could see the car was running and the headlights were on. I grabbed for the door handle of the front passenger side and found it locked.

"Lisa!" I screamed, pounding on the window. "Lisa, open up! It's Gary!"

I heard Lisa fumbling with the lock as I yanked at the handle again. The rest of the doors unlocked, but I'd pulled at the wrong moment and my door remained closed.

"Again!" I shouted to Lisa.

In the longest second I'd ever lived through, Lisa leaned across and flicked open the lock for my door with her hand. Cliff and Diane had already slammed into the back seat by the time I made it into the front.

"Floor it!" Diane commanded from the back.

Lisa slammed the car into gear with shaking hands and gunned it, the rear of the car fishtailing wildly for a moment before the tires gained traction. I glanced toward the bridge and saw a grotesque, dog-headed figure floating on the far side, watching us. In a second, it disappeared behind a screen of trees as the car shot off down the road, seeming to hit every pothole as Lisa raced for home.

"I saw it!" Lisa cried through chattering teeth as she drove frantically down the rugged road. "I saw the bright light coming toward me down the road, just like in the story. I thought I was dead, but it vanished just before it reached the car!"

"Well, we saw the dog-headed woman," Diane said from the backseat.

At that, Jill nearly drove off the road in panic. I caught the wheel of the car just in time and steered us back into the center.

"Don't freak out the driver," Cliff scolded his girlfriend. "You nearly got us killed."

After what seemed like ages, we reached the main road, and everyone relaxed, more or less. We didn't talk much on the return trip. I think we all had had enough of a scare for one Halloween.

14

Diamond Ring

NEWBURGH

It was a fine diamond ring . . . a mighty fine diamond ring. It flashed and sparkled on the hand of the old farmer's wife as she hurried back and forth setting dishes onto the long serving tables on the lawn of the church.

On that sunny August day in the late 1880s, the church was having its annual picnic. It was a grand occasion. So many folks had come in wagons and buggies and on foot and bicycles that there was hardly room to move about. The benches around the picnic tables were so full that families were eating in shifts. Several church folks were playing music on fiddles, guitars, and other instruments. The reverend was wandering through the crowd with a kind word for everyone. And the grandmother was helping out with a brand new diamond ring gleaming on her wrinkled old hand.

The townsfolk weren't too rich in those days, with nary a dime to spare on extras. So the ring was quite a novelty item to many. The women gathered around the grandmother to ooh and ahh over the diamond ring and to give advice on the best way to keep it clean. The old farmer had worked hard to put that diamond ring on his old wife's hand. Now, he stood listening to the chatter, beaming in delight.

The Jackson brothers were smiling, too, but not in a neighborly way. You see, the Jackson brothers were trouble. They liked money—oh yes, they did—but they didn't like working for it. When they saw that diamond ring on the grandmother's hand, they wanted it. They wanted it bad.

"We gotta get that ring," the elder Jackson said to his brother. "We could sell it for a bundle and live the good life."

"We could afford to go to California!" the younger Jackson agreed enthusiastically. "How much do you think it cost the old man?"

"I dunno, but I'm gonna find out," the elder Jackson said.

He wandered casually over to the granddad and started talking to him about the weather, crops, and raising horses. The old farmer was pleasantly surprised by this attention from the normally sullen young man.

Then, Jackson said: "I was thinking of proposing to my best gal. I'd like to give her a ring like the one your wife is wearing. Would you sell it to me?"

The granddad's face wrinkled with disgust. He knew very well the Jackson boy wasn't courting anyone at present and had no money for a ring. He was just fishing for information in a vulgar manner that the granddad deplored. "The ring is not for sale," he said with dignity, and walked away.

The elder Jackson glared after him. Who did that snobby old man think he was, treating a Jackson with such rudeness! He marched back to his brother, muttering under his breath. He would have that diamond ring, and it would pay for a better life for him and his brother. Oh, yes.

DIAMOND RING

The Jackson boys made every excuse they could to drop by the old farmer's house, hoping to steal the diamond ring the second she took it off. To no avail. It never left her hand. The grandmother wore the ring to bed, when she bathed, and even when she made bread, turning the diamond toward her palm so the sticky dough wouldn't pull it loose.

The Jacksons were about to give up their get-rich-quick scheme when the old lady suddenly fell ill and passed away. They were overjoyed at the news. They figured the granddad would put his wife's diamond away somewhere safe, and they'd slip in while he was out tending stock and steal it. They'd be on a train for California long before he knew it was gone.

The Jackson brothers went to the grandmother's funeral, hoping to discover the fate of the diamond ring. Would the old man keep it himself or give it to one of his children? They were so impatient to interview the chief mourners that they hardly heard a word of the memorial service. As they went up to pay their last respects, the eyes of the younger Jackson fell on the corpse.

"It's there!" he gasped, grabbing his brother's arm. "He left it on her finger!"

The elder Jackson looked at the old lady and frowned in dismay. The diamond still glittered on her wrinkled hand. The farmer was going to bury it with her!

"Bad. That's bad," said the younger brother.

The elder Jackson hushed him. "Not so bad," he murmured back. "In fact, it's positively ideal."

The younger brother looked at him curiously and then realized what he meant. After the old lady was buried, no one would notice if her ring went missing. He smothered a chuckle and composed his face into a suitably mournful expression as the elder Jackson steered him toward the granddad, standing near the casket with his grown daughter and son.

Late that night, the Jackson brothers snuck back into the churchyard carrying two shovels and a lantern. They commenced digging out the loosened dirt that covered the newly buried casket. It was heavy, hot work, but greed spurred them onward. After a long, sticky interval, they cleared the lid of the casket and pried it open. The old lady lay serenely inside, eyes closed, wrinkled hands folded so the diamond ring was on top. Jackson, the elder, gave a greedy grunt and tugged at the old lady's hand with his dirty paw, determined to wrench off the prize and bear it away. But the diamond ring was stuck on her finger. He couldn't get it off.

"Let me try," the younger Jackson said impatiently.

He tugged and pulled, dislodging a quantity of dirt upon the lined face of the poor deceased grandmother. If the boy had chanced to look at her face in the dim light of the lantern, he might have noticed it was no longer serene. A tiny frown had formed on her wide mouth. But neither Jackson noticed.

"We'll have to cut it off," the elder Jackson said, pulling out his knife.

"Won't that be bloody?" asked the younger boy.

"Dunno. Don't care," said the elder Jackson.

Then he commenced to sawing at the old lady's finger . . . and the old lady screamed and sat straight up in her coffin! The two brothers reeled back in horror as her blue eyes opened and glared at them accusingly. When she screamed again and clutched her injured finger, the Jacksons scrambled up and out of the grave in a panic. Their screams were even louder than those of the grandmother.

"Haints! Ghosts! Zombies!" the younger Jackson shouted, his feet seeming to take wing.

"She's done rose from the dead to punish us fer stealing her ring," roared the elder Jackson.

The brothers made tracks for the nearest railroad station and leapt aboard an empty coal car of the first passing train. They were never seen again.

Back in the graveyard, the grandmother climbed shakily out of her casket, pulled herself out of the hole, and walked home. Her husband nearly had a heart attack when he opened his door around midnight and saw his dead wife standing there with her bleeding finger and dirt-stained clothes. The whole family was staying overnight, and they screamed and hollered in terror, thinking she was a ghost. Then, they laughed and cried and thanked the good Lord for those two wretched Jackson boys, who'd saved the life of their grandmother, whom they'd accidentally buried alive.

15

Bloody Mary Whales

LAKE COUNTY

Old Man Whales was a nineteenth-century farmer who loved money more than anything, except his wife. In his lust for wealth, he supplemented his farm income by catching runaway slaves who were escaping to freedom through Indiana. Whales would chain the ex-slaves up in his barn cellar until he could collect the reward on them, and when he couldn't find slaves, he'd capture free men and sell them into slavery. Whales hated just about every human being on Earth except for his Virginia. She was a gentle soul who lived in fear of her stern husband, though she loved him devotedly and had no idea how much he cherished her in return, for he was not a demonstrative man.

Then, things changed. The Civil War ended slavery—a disaster for the evil Whales, who no longer had a profitable source of income to supplement his farm work—and Virginia died in childbirth. Overnight, Whales fell to pieces. He hated the child—a little girl his wife had named Mary—but he raised her for Virginia's sake. As for himself, he withdrew from the world, neglecting his farm and half-starving his child.

Mary was a beautiful girl with lovely blond curls falling in a tangle down her back. She dressed in filthy rags, and when she was in town, she never spoke to anyone except her sullen, angry father. Old Man Whales somehow scratched out a living from his farm—enough to keep himself and his daughter alive. But he took to drinking heavily as the years went by, and Mary did most of the farm work as well as all the cooking and housekeeping.

Whenever she had a moment, Mary escaped into books, where she found a fantasy world much more to her liking than the world she lived in. Sometimes, she wondered if she could do anything to win her father's affection. She tried so hard, but he remained cruel and distant, and his loathing became increasingly more apparent as she grew older. Unbeknownst to the girl, she grew ever lovelier as she neared adulthood, and the resemblance to her dead mother was striking. Whales saw his dead wife every time he looked at the child who had caused her death.

One night, after a hefty bout of drinking, Whales stumbled home with an aching head and a black rage in his heart over the cruelty of a world that would deprive him of Virginia. The person at fault for this dastardly crime lay sleeping peacefully in her bed, and Whales could not stand the thought. Grabbing the knife he used to slaughter his pigs, Whales lumbered into Mary's bedroom and stabbed her to death, flailing at her repeatedly as if she were an attacking bear rather than a sleeping girl. Mary woke screaming and thrashed around in agony, trying to fight off her demonic father as blood spurted everywhere and bits of torn flesh littered the bedclothes and fell to the floor. When she stopped moving, Whales reeled out of the room in satisfaction, leaving a bloody corpse in his wake. Mary's head was nearly severed, and her body lay half-on and half-off the bed, her ragged dress covered in gore, while hanks of her blonde hair trailed in the pool of blood accumulating on the floor beneath her bed.

BLOODY MARY WHALES

When Old Man Whales woke the next morning, his head finally clear of the whisky-induced haze, he staggered into the bedroom to inspect his work. The sight of his bloody Mary brought a demonic smile to his lips. He should have killed her years ago, he decided. But she'd made quite a mess, and he didn't want the tramp littering up his house, not even in death. So he slung Mary over his shoulder and carried her down to the basement, where he'd once kept captured slaves. He dug an indifferent grave and tossed her body into it. And that was the end of Mary . . . or so he thought.

Two nights later, when Old Man Whales came back from doing his nightly chores at the barn, he found Mary standing in the kitchen, her nearly severed head lolling against one shoulder as she stirred an empty kettle. A pool of steaming blood lay beneath her feet, and bits of skin from her knife-slashed face were breaking off and falling into the kettle. Old Man Whales screamed and reeled backward in shock.

At the sound, Bloody Mary looked up from her stirring, and a smile crossed her knife-split mouth, widening until it showed shattered teeth. "Faaaaaather . . ." she hissed, and launched herself across the room at her father, the wooden spoon in her hand held like a knife.

Old Man Whales leapt backward out of the kitchen door and fled to the barn. When he chanced a look over his shoulder, the apparition was gone. He spent a sleepless the night in the barn, fortifying himself with a keg of whisky he kept there for emergencies.

In the morning, he staggered into the house carrying his axe for protection. The house was in its customary squalor, and there was no bloody pool on the kitchen floor. The kettle hung demurely from its iron hook at the side of the hearth. Old Man Whales sucked in a terrified breath, and then relaxed. He'd probably been drunk last night and imagined the whole thing, he decided, forgetting he hadn't started drinking until after he'd seen Bloody Mary.

A week passed. Old Man Whales went about his chores whistling cheerfully, feeling better than he had in years. He brought a newspaper home from the mercantile and sat down by the hearth in the chair he'd favored when Virginia was alive to read it.

As he turned to page two, he glanced up and saw Bloody Mary sitting in the chair opposite him, her knife-slashed dress covered in blood. Her pale skin was shattered by knife blows, the cuts raw and bleeding, and her sliced-up hands were busy knitting him a shirt. She had to jerk her half-severed head sideways to look at him with eyes that glowed red with hatred. "Faaaaaather . . ." she hissed through knife-scored lips. Then, she smiled, showing all of her broken teeth, now razor-sharp points that bit down on a tattered tongue. Blood pooled under her chair and fell from her body like rain as she flew across the room toward him, knitting needles held like knives.

Old Man Whales screamed and reeled away, his chair smashing to the floor as he fled from the house. He felt a slashing pain across his back as he leapt through the back door. It was only when he'd safely reached the barn that he stopped to assess the damage. His shirt was in tatters, and two long gashes scored deeply into his back, like the cuts of a butcher's knife . . . or two sharpened knitting needles.

The murderous widower did not go back into the house for days. He slept in the barn and cooked meals around a bonfire he built in the pasture where he kept his cows. Then, he grew tired of this nonsense. It was all his imagination. Too much whisky before bed, he told himself. He allowed himself only one drink before bedding down in the barn that night, and in the morning he marched straight up the weedy walkway and into his house. He'd get cleaned up, shave, and go to town this morning, he decided. It was time he took his place in the community once more.

So he pumped himself a bucket of water at the kitchen sink, washed up, and then took an ewer of water over to the little mirror kept on the far wall for shaving. He set it down on the table and looked into the mirror . . . right into the glowing red eyes of Bloody Mary. Her shattered face was knife scored, her once-fair lips were split down the center, and blood dripped from them as she smiled at him. "Faaaaaather . . ." she hissed through razor-sharp, blood-stained teeth. A piece of her lip broke off and fell out of sight below the bottom of the mirror as she spoke. She raised blood-stained fingers, her nails long and sharpened like the claws of a beast, and reached right out of the mirror toward her father; slapping him twice across the face.

Old Man Whales screamed in searing pain as her nails clawed into him, and blood streamed from four slashes, two on either cheek, as he ran from the house toward the safety of the barn. He leapt through the door of the barn, his heart pounding so hard his chest ached with it. He swiped at his bloody cheeks as if wiping away tears, panting desperately. The dust from the hay bales in the loft above tickled his nose, and he sneezed, eyes streaming. He swiped at his eyes with his bloody hand, and they stung as gore leaked into them. "Tramp. Bloody witch," he shouted, half-blinded by blood, tears, and fear.

"Faaaaaather . . ." a voice hissed softly behind him.

Old Man Whales whirled around with a shriek. Blood Mary stood smiling at him through her bloody, razor-sharp teeth, her tattered tongue bleeding from several places, as if it had been scored by a butcher's knife. Her head listed to one side as blood streamed from the wound that had nearly decapitated her. The viscous pool of steaming blood at her feet flowed slowly toward him. She pointed above her head.

Her murderous father lifted his stunned eyes and saw a noose hanging from the rafters beside the ladder to the loft. The rope looked inviting, hanging there in a dust-speckled sunbeam. Hanging there so peaceful and still. Old Man Whales stepped forward and placed his bloody hands on the rung of the ladder. He started to climb. . . .

16

The Dance

Marie Elise was furious with her beau for being late, tonight of all nights. It was the night of the big holiday dance, and her beau had promised he would pick her up in his sleigh an hour before the party started so she could dance every dance. He'd promised! Here it was nearly eight o'clock, and the dance started at eight thirty. And still no sign of him!

She glared at the clock, and then went back to the mirror to straighten her hair.

"If you'd stop pacing, your hair would stay in place," her mother called from the fireside chair. She was knitting placidly, ignoring her daughter's anger.

Marie Elise frowned at her mother and started pacing back and forth across the sitting room, her long skirts swirling against the carpet as she stalked to and fro. "I will never forgive Ned for making us late to the dance!" she exclaimed as she paced. "Never, never, never!"

"You are acting like a two-year-old child," her mother remarked, turning the heel on the sock she was knitting. "Has it occurred to you that Ned might not be coming tonight?"

Her daughter stopped in her tracks, her pretty red mouth dropping open in shock. "Not coming? Of course he's coming! I'm the prettiest girl in school, and he's the handsomest boy. He'd never go to the dance with someone else!"

Her mother eyed her wryly. She and her husband had made a mistake in spoiling Marie Elise. They had indulged her too much as a child and now were repenting it. She was vain as a kitten, and her head was empty of everything but frills and frocks and boys. She expected everyone and everything to fall in with her plans, and she threw a tantrum anytime something didn't go her way.

"I meant that it is extremely cold tonight, and snow is falling," her mother said. "Ned might not be able to make it through the storm."

"Of course he can! What's a little cold and snow compared to the wonders of the dance!" Marie Elise whirled around the room, demonstrating a fancy waltz turn as she spoke.

"Anyway, I don't care if Ned comes or not," she added with a pout of her red lips. "I would go to the dance with anyone who will take me. I'd even go with the devil himself, if he asked me politely. Just so long as I go to the dance!"

"Marie Elise! Watch your tongue!" Her mother was shocked. She'd raised her daughter to be a God-fearing, church-going young woman. Such talk of the devil was sacrilegious. And maybe even dangerous, a tiny voice murmured at the back of her mind.

"I wouldn't mind if the devil did take me to the dance," Marie Elise said boldly. "It would make me stand out from the other girls."

Before her mother could remonstrate further, they heard the sound of sleigh bells approaching. Marie Elise exclaimed excitedly and ran to look out the window into the snowy lane. Approaching the house was an elegant sleigh pulled by two midnight-black horses that looked like ink blots against the white snow.

"Oh! Ned has rented a fancy sleigh for the night," Marie Elise cried happily. "I told you he wouldn't take anyone else to the dance. He knows I'm the prettiest girl in school. In the whole county! Maybe in the whole state!"

She danced around the room for a moment, long skirts swirling about her. Then, she ran to get her cloak and her muff as footsteps sounded on the porch and the knocker rapped against the front door.

"Get the door, Mother," Marie Elise called as she scrambled into her outdoor clothing.

Her mother sighed, put down her knitting, and went to the door. She opened it with a smile, for she rather liked Ned, who was always polite to her and her hard-working husband. The open door revealed a very handsome stranger standing on the stoop with hat in his hand, snowflakes melting on his dark, curly hair.

"Good evening," the mother said politely. "May I help you?"

Before the stranger could speak, the mother was shoved rudely aside by Marie Elise, who exclaimed: "I won't forgive you for being so late, Ned Bl—"

Marie Elise stopped in midsentence when she saw the stranger, who reached past her to steady her poor mother, who'd fallen against the doorframe.

"Who are you?" Marie Elise cried rudely. Then, she blinked, realizing this dark stranger was twice as handsome as Ned. She primed her long, gold curls and added in her sweetest tone, "Can I help you with something? Are you lost?"

"Not lost. I am here on behalf of Ned," the dark-haired, dark-eyed charmer said smoothly. "He was called away to see a dying relative and asked me to take you to the dance tonight in his place. He didn't want to disappoint you."

"How very kind of him," gurgled Marie Elise. "And even kinder of you." She cooed the last three words and then stepped out on the porch to take his arm.

In the doorway, her mother frowned. "What is your name, sir? Who are your folks?" she asked. "Won't you come in and let us get to know you better? Marie Elise, we should invite him in to warm up."

The mother stared keenly at the stranger, feeling uneasy. His hand, when he steadied her, had been too warm. His touch had nearly burnt her, even through the thick layers of her winter dress. And there was a red glint in his eye that she did not like. Her daughter had just invoked the name of the devil, and now here was this stranger standing on their doorstep with his reddish eyes and haughty smile and hot skin.

"Mother! Don't fuss," Marie Elise exclaimed, flushing with anger, her pretty red lips pursed sourly.

"*You* have nothing to fear, Madam," the stranger said with an odd smile.

Was she the only one who heard the emphasis on the first word, the mother wondered?

"Marie Elise. Remember what you have just said," the mother said, reaching desperately for her daughter.

Marie Elise stepped away, glaring at her mother with real hatred in her blue eyes. "I said it once, and I'll say it again," the young woman said tartly. "I am going to the dance no matter what. I'd even go with the devil himself, if he asked me politely. Just so long as I go to the dance."

"And will you accompany me tonight, my fair lady?" asked the stranger with a charming smile and a bow.

"Sir, I will," Marie Elise replied with an equally charming smile.

Then, the young woman curtseyed, turned her back upon her mother, and walked with her escort down the steps and out to the waiting sleigh. The mother stared fearfully after her daughter, and when Marie Elise stepped up into the seat and drove away with the strange man to the tintinnabulation of sleigh bells, she buried her face in her hands and wept.

Marie Elise exclaimed excitedly over the fancy sleigh, the fine midnight-black horses, and the falling snow, so pretty and delicate. The handsome stranger laughed and spoke sweetly to the girl of fancy balls attended, far-off places visited, and exotic sights seen. The trees flashed by in the light of the carriage lanterns, blurring slightly with their speed. Marie Elise had never had a merrier sleigh-ride. Her escort was so charming, so handsome, so debonair. Ned was nothing compared to him.

As the air grew colder and still colder, Marie Elise hugged her cloak around her. She snuggled her hands deeper into the fleece and edged a bit nearer to her escort for warmth. The handsome man was warm, very warm . . . the only warm thing on this cold, cold night.

The sleigh twisted and turned down the long, windy road, and Marie Elise's breath turned to frost with every exhalation. Yet, the heat emanating from her escort made the seat uncomfortable to sit on, and the side of Marie Elise closest to

THE DANCE

the stranger was extremely hot, as if she were sitting next to a roaring fire. She edged away from him until she was pressed against the frigid side of the sleigh. Now, one side of her was freezing cold and the other side was too hot.

"Sir," she exclaimed suddenly, realizing belatedly that they had traveled a long distance without arriving at their destination. "I believe we must be lost. The dance cannot be this far out in the country."

"Lost?" the man said in a deep voice that echoed with the crackle and spit of flames. "No, we are not lost, Marie Elisssssse." He hissed the final syllable of her name like a snake, and when he turned to look at her, the red glow of his eyes lit the seat. The bare skin of her face heated painfully and tightened across her bones as if she'd spent too much time in the sun.

"I am taking you to the dance," the man continued as she stared, hypnotized, into his blazing eyes. "My dance!"

Marie Elise's hair and clothes caught fire from the unbearable heat pulsing from the man beside her. The devil laughed as she screamed in agony. Then devil, sleigh, and horses vanished, and Marie Elise, her body aflame, fell down, down, down into a looming black pit that ended far, far below . . . in brimstone.

17

Fireball

HUNTINGTON COUNTY

It was midwinter 1905, and Murrell and I were walking home from school, swinging our lunch pails and discussing the mathematics homework our teacher had set for us that afternoon. The snow drifted deeply on either side, though the lane itself was a clear, icy space with the occasional rut where horses' hooves or a sleigh runner had dug in too deeply.

"I just don't understand the word problems," Murrell complained. "They are too complicated. And we have a test on Monday. I know I'll fail it."

"You won't fail," I assured her, brushing a strand of dark hair off my face. My curly hair was always escaping its braid. It drove me wild. "I'll come over tomorrow and help you study."

Murrell's face lit up. "Will you, Anne?" she cried. "Thanks!"

I smiled at her. She was one of my nearest neighbors and a good friend. She'd helped me piece a quilt last summer when Mama had assigned me the chore. I loathed sewing, and I'd much appreciated Murrell's quick fingers and cheerful chatter. It made the quilting bearable. I felt I owed her something for all the trouble she'd taken with the quilt last summer, and here was my chance to repay her.

We had reached Murrell's house by this time. Murrell paused beside the gate to bid me farewell and then stiffened. "Anne, look," she gasped, pointing behind her house.

I followed the line of her finger and saw a huge ball of fire whirling frantically away from the back door, heading toward the woods. As it reached the edge of her property, it suddenly vanished.

"What was that?" gasped Murrell, her face going pale.

"I don't know," I replied shakily, clutching the fence rail with my trembling hand and forcing my wobbly knees to hold me upright.

My stomach lurched as I replayed the scene in my mind. I'd heard—at least, I thought I'd heard—a child screaming from the center of the giant fireball. That couldn't be right. Of course not!

"Perhaps we imagined it," I said, trying to reassure myself as much as Murrell.

Murrell's face darkened with sudden conviction. "It was an omen," she said. "Something terrible is going to happen."

"Don't be silly," I said in a voice that trembled too much to reassure.

"I must tell Mother," Murrell said. "I will see you tomorrow, Anne."

She rushed down the shoveled path and fled into the house. I wasn't quite sure what she thought her mother could do about the strange fireball we'd seen. Her mother had been very ill ever since the new baby had been born ten days ago. She could barely sit up in a chair for more than a half hour at a time before retreating to her bed. She could not be expected to investigate disappearing fireballs.

I walked home slowly, my gut shaken by the strange experience. But I forgot all about it when a snowball crashed into my shoulder as I turned into my driveway. My elder brother grinned at me from the front lawn, tossing another snowball up and down in his gloved hands. I dropped my books immediately and armed myself, all thoughts of disappearing fireballs forgotten in my hasty preparation for a snow war.

I finished my chores early the next morning, and Mama gave me permission to walk to Murrell's house to study. I whistled cheerfully as I slipped and slid down the icy lane, swinging my satchel full of schoolbooks. I slowed as I neared Murrell's house, watching for mysteriously vanishing fireballs, but the only burning object I saw was the sun way up in the sky. Oh no, my mistake: There was a fire . . . near the pigpen. As I drew closer, I saw that it was Murrell's father boiling up some potatoes in a large kettle hanging over an open fire, making swill for the pigs. He smiled and waved when he saw me.

"Good morning, Anne," he said pleasantly. "Murrell's in the house helping her ma."

"Thank you, Mr. Meyers," I said with an answering smile.

I entered the house to find things in a state of mild chaos. The baby was screaming, Mrs. Meyers was lying down with a sick headache, and little Tony had just knocked over the butter churn, spilling curds everywhere. I scooped up the sobbing two-year-old and held him on my lap while Murrell cleaned up the mess. The other children, four and six years old respectively, peered down at us from the loft, where Murrell had banished them for shouting and giving their mama a sore head.

Mr. Meyers poked his head in at this juncture and called to Murrell. "I am going out to the clearing to harvest those trees I marked the other day. I reckon they will make enough lumber to build the addition to the house come spring. Keep the children away from the pig's swill pot."

Murrell nodded a distracted acknowledgment from her place on the floor. She was still mopping up the spilled milk as Mr. Meyers kissed his ailing wife and departed. I put the squirming Tony down on the bed beside his baby brother and his mother, and then I went to fix Mrs. Meyers some willow bark tea, which was good for headaches. Within fifteen minutes, the house was serene again. The older children were allowed downstairs to play in the sitting room with Tony, while Murrell and I did our mathematics problems around the kitchen table. The tea revived Mrs. Meyers so much that she got up and started kneading the dough Murrell had set to rise very early that morning.

It was quarter to eleven when Mrs. Meyers exclaimed, "Why Joseph has forgotten his lunch!"

Murrell and I both looked up from our books and saw the lunch pail on the sideboard. "I'll take it to him, Mama," said Murrell, standing up and stretching out the kinks.

At that moment, there came a thud and then a boy's angry roar from the sitting room. The children were quarrelling.

Mrs. Meyer sighed and said, "Please go sort that out, Murrell. Anne can take the lunch to your papa."

Murrell made a face but went obediently into the front room to scold her siblings into good behavior. I donned my coat and snow boots, got directions to the clearing from Mrs. Meyers, and headed out the back door into the snow.

FIREBALL

The potatoes were boiling nicely in the big black kettle that hung over the fire beside the pigpen. It smelled rather tasty, though I knew the swill was good only for pigs. I tramped past the pigpen and the fire, feeling the warmth of the blaze from several feet away. Then I followed Mr. Meyers' footprints through the woods, up and over a small ridge, and then down into a clearing near the stream.

Mr. Meyers looked up when I entered the clearing. He was chopping a newly fallen tree into easy-to-haul pieces—a heavy job—and greeted the sight of the lunch pail with a smile.

"Bless Emily for remembering! That will save me a half hour," he said. He thanked me, too, and asked me to set the lunch pail down on the new stump.

I tromped back up the ridge and down the other side, enjoying the lovely, cold day. It was hard work walking in deep snow, but the mix of sun and tree shadows on the snow made lovely, lacy pictures, and sparkles from the ice crystals danced here and there.

All too soon, I reached the edge of the woods, stepped out into the back yard, and saw a fireball hurling toward me across the snow! I gasped in alarm and ducked. Then, I realized it wasn't a fireball. It was a small child, clothes ablaze, racing through the snow toward me as if he were trying to outrun the flames that enveloped him from shoe to collar. He was screaming in agony. As soon as my mind registered what I was seeing, I screamed, too. I was twenty yards away from little Tony, and I ran as fast as I could toward the burning child.

"Lay down," I shouted desperately to the two-year-old. "Lay down and roll!"

The back door burst open as I shouted. Murrell and her mother came rushing out to see what the noise was about. They'd been busy treating a bloody scrape the six-year-old had received during the tussle in the front room and hadn't even noticed Tony had gone outside. Their screams mingled with little Tony's wail as they took in the situation and ran toward the blazing toddler.

The three of us reached the toddler at the same time, thrusting him down into the snow and rolling him around, frantically trying to douse the flames. Tony's screams turned to a tiny, sobbing moan that died away with the flames. His body was burnt black with raw red patches where his clothes had protected him a mite. Only his shoes and the collar of his shirt remained.

Sobbing, Mrs. Meyers attempted to lift Tony up, but she was still weak from her recent childbirth and fell on her knees, his little burnt body clutched to her chest.

With a shout from the edge of the woods, Mr. Meyers raced toward us, his eyes wide with fear. "I heard screams! What's wrong?" he cried.

Then he saw the little, unmoving body in his wife's arms. Tony was still breathing, but barely. Mr. Meyers picked up the burnt child with one large hand and cradled him against his broad shoulder. With his other hand, he helped his wife up. While Murrell ran for the doctor, I raced into the house to prepare every home remedy I had learned of to treat Tony's burns. It was already too late, I knew, somewhere deep in my mind. But we had to try. All of us had to try.

Little Tony died an hour later, shortly after the doctor arrived. Mrs. Meyers fell into her husband's arms, weeping desperately. Murrell rushed out the back door, and I followed, feeling terrible. If only I hadn't lingered in the woods. If only I had hurried right back after giving Mr. Meyers his lunch. If only . . . Mama said those were the two saddest words in the whole world. Now, I knew what she meant.

Murrell turned a tear-streaked face to me and pointed toward the edge of the house. "The fireball," she whispered. "The fireball."

I followed the line of her finger, suddenly realizing that little Tony, in his death throes, had run along the path taken by the vanishing fireball we'd seen yesterday. The fireball had been an omen foretelling his death by fire. Swallowing in horror, I stared back at my friend.

"Was there something we could have done?" I asked her.

I waited for her answer, throat going dry with dread. The answer came not from Murrell, who was weeping again, but from Mr. Meyers, who stood in the doorway. His dark eyes were wet with grief.

"There was nothing you could do, child. Nothing any of us could do," he said firmly. "It was an accident. Tony didn't listen to his Mama or Murrell when they told him to stay in the house. He slipped outside while they were fixing up little Hannah's knee. It wasn't anyone's fault."

I nodded and put my arm around the weeping Murrell, and Mr. Meyers went back into the house. I thought about the fireball as I comforted my friend. What was the use of a death omen when you didn't know what it meant until it was too late? Were these tragedies inevitable? Could they be turned aside somehow, if the family understood the warning? I didn't know the answers to my questions, but I swore at that moment that I would discover the truth. If death omens could be used to prevent tragedies, instead of just foreshadowing them, then I owed it to Tony—and to myself—to find out.

With that decided, I urged my weeping friend to come inside the house and drink some tea.

18

Loup-Garou

EVANSVILLE

He sat at the bar in the inn. It was early fall in the year of our Lord 1880, and the hunter was drinking whisky and listening to rumors as the sun set on Evansville. It was a rumor that had brought him to town on that particular night. According to the story he'd heard, some kind of wild animal was stalking people near the graveyard at the edge of town. The animal reportedly looked like an overgrown wolf, but unlike a wolf, it did not flee when confronted by guns or fire, both of which had been used in an effort to frighten off the fell creature. Bullets seemed to have no effect upon it, and the only way to escape its sharp teeth was to flee as fast as possible in the opposite direction.

More than one traveler had appeared at the local inn with ripped clothing and bite marks upon arms and legs where the menacing creature had harassed them. The town had raised a hunt in an effort to eradicate the menace, but hunters could do little about a creature that was impervious to bullets.

Now, a month after the first sighting of the creature, the town was in a panic. Parents kept little children inside at night, and folks found alternate routes rather than pass the graveyard at any time of day.

From the descriptions he'd heard, the hunter knew at once that the creature was a *loup-garou*. According to his French Canadian grandmother, loup-garous (or werewolves, as they're known in English), were men who had neglected their religious duties for so long that they had fallen under the spell of the devil, who turned them into wolves and forced them to do his bidding. His *grandpère*, on the other hand, told him that loup-garous were a more natural phenomenon—humans born with the ability to shape-shift at will. However, both his grandparents agreed on one point: The only way to defeat a werewolf was to cut him with a silver knife blade, which returned the loup-garou to his human shape. They had given their grandson a knife with a silver blade as a Christmas gift when he was ten years old, and he'd carried it with him ever since, in the top of his right boot.

The hunter sipped his whiskey thoughtfully as several of the local men waxed eloquently over the creature's size and fierceness. To hear them, you might well believe it was as large as a baby elephant with teeth sharper than a grizzly bear and the speed of a galloping horse.

Their descriptions were as vague as their directions. The creature had been seen on the north side of town. No, no, it was last seen on the south side of town, near the graveyard. Which graveyard? There was no graveyard over there. Do you mean the cemetery to the east of the mercantile? No, the one across town. And so forth.

The hunter paid for his whiskey and asked a big, red-bearded fellow if there was a bounty on the mysterious creature. Oh yes, the man said, a big reward was offered for the body of the beast. The hunter nodded thoughtfully and headed outside with his rifle. If the creature really was a loup-garou, the gun wouldn't do him any good, but the creature might just be a wily old wolf that was smarter than the folks who hunted it. That was the problem with rumors. You couldn't tell if they were true until you confronted the beast in question. And, by golly, you'd better be prepared for anything—from a baby elephant with sharp teeth that moved like a horse, to a wily wolf with a bad temper, to an evil loup-garou. A gun would work in two of those cases, and his silver knife would take care of the third.

The hunter headed slowly down the lantern-lit avenue and then turned toward the back streets, wandering through every graveyard in town, hoping to lure out the beast. He was a patient man. He'd walk every inch of Evansville every night until he found the creature. It didn't pay to be in a hurry, and a panicked hunter was a dead hunter, in his experience.

As he meandered slowly through the dark streets, the hunter wondered why the loup-garou had chosen to haunt this particular place. Had someone laid a curse upon the town? He hadn't heard of any witches living in Evansville, and to his knowledge, there weren't any disastrous wars with the natives in the region that might have resulted in a medicine man's curse. Perhaps it was a private family matter? Were the victims of the loup-garou all related somehow?

Absentmindedly, he turned into a lane lined with apple trees that led by an old graveyard. It was very dark, rather cold, and silent . . . too silent. The hunter went on the alert at once. There were no sounds at all, save for his soft footfalls on the dirt road and the occasional thud as he accidentally kicked a fallen apple. No creatures stirred. No insects buzzed or chirruped. No swish of wings from a bat or a night bird. Even the wind was still. He had his gun cocked and ready when a nightmarish figure

LOUP-GAROU

suddenly leapt over the iron fence surrounding the graveyard. He pulled the trigger as the animal jumped on him, knocking his gun aside.

The hunter thrust his hands desperately upward and closed them around the creature's neck, barely keeping its teeth from his jugular vein. Man and beast rolled over and over in the dusty lane, the hunter on top, then the beast on top, then the hunter on top . . . The smell of crushed apples filled the air as their bodies crushed the fallen fruit, and hard lumps of apple bruised the hunter's back as he struggled for his life.

The creature's claws scrabbled at the hunter's jacket and pants, ripping through the heavy cloth and scraping his skin. Its stinking, hot breath gagged him as the beast snarled and struggled to loosen itself. It had the general shape of a wolf, the hunter noted grimly, as he rolled again to maneuver his way to the top of the creature. He forced it down into the dirt with all his weight and pressed hard against its neck, cutting off its breath. The beast squirmed and snapped desperately, its teeth inches from his face. But the creature was slowly strangling, and its struggles grew feebler as the breath was choked out of it.

The hunter took a chance and freed one hand momentarily to grab the silver knife from his boot. The moment of truth was at hand. In one swift gesture, he whipped out the knife and drew it across the creature's neck just below his stranglehold. Blood gushed onto his clothing. And then, the creature began to change. . . .

Its whole body writhed strangely, stretching out in some places and condensing in others. The transformation felt so strange beneath the hunter's panting, sweating body that he rolled off the beast and watched in the dim moonlight filtering through the leaves of the apple trees. He held his knife ready for whatever was to come, tensed to leap upon the horribly stretching thing on the ground in front of him. Finally, it solidified and became a naked man lying facedown, covered in dirt and squashed bits of apple.

The naked man lifted his head slowly, and the hunter saw blood trickling from a cut on his neck.

"Who are you, loup-garou?" the hunter demanded. "Why are you plaguing this town?"

The man sat up and put his hand over his bleeding neck. "I am no one, now," he said bitterly. "Once, I had a good job, happiness, a wife, and family. Then I was framed for murder. I stood trial and was acquitted, but when I came home, I found my job had been taken away, my family had disowned me, and my wife had run away with a man from Evansville, taking my only child with her. I tried to get custody of the child, but the courts would have nothing to do with me. So I . . . made a deal with the devil."

The loup-garou turned his dark eyes away from the hunter, half-defiant, half-ashamed. "I became a loup-garou and brought terror to the people of Evansville, hoping to drive my wife and her paramour away from town. I planned to steal my child out of his carriage when they fled and take the boy to his grandparents in Canada. Now, I do not know what I shall do."

He turned toward the hunter again, his eyes blazing. "Kill me! Put me out of my misery! You can do it. You have the knife."

The hunter felt pity stir within him. Slowly, he sheathed the knife and said, "Leave this place, loup-garou. Go home to Canada. Or go west, to the mountains or California. Take a new wife and have more sons. I will give you one more chance to redeem yourself."

"Redeem myself!" the man spat angrily. But there was a note in his voice that told the hunter he wished to be persuaded. "I sold my soul to the devil to become what I am."

"And my knife has brought you a second chance," the hunter said calmly. "If you remain a man for a year and a day, you buy your freedom."

"Only if you do not speak of me to any man during that time," the loup-garou said bitterly. "We must both be silent, or the spell will remain upon me for all time."

"I will not speak, if you will leave this place," the hunter said. "If I see you again, in any form, I will finish the work my knife began."

The loup-garou hesitated for a long moment. Then, he nodded silently.

"Now go," said the hunter. "Go, and do not return!"

The loup-garou slunk off into the graveyard without another word.

The hunter watched his retreat, wondering if he'd done the right thing. He'd always trusted his instincts in the past, and they'd never led him wrong. His instinct now was to let the man go in peace to find a new life for himself, even though it meant sacrificing the reward. Perhaps it would turn out all right in the end. A good deed was supposed to be its own reward, right?

In the meantime, he'd stick around Evansville for a week, just to make sure the loup-garou was truly gone. No use in taking chances. The hunter slipped the silver knife into his boot, picked up his rifle, and headed back to the inn, whistling cheerfully.

19

Three Fawns

SHELBY COUNTY

In July of 1850, shortly after my wife died, I moved into town with my young daughter, Matilda. At the time, there were plenty of stories circulating about three witches who had recently built a log cabin in the woods just outside town. I didn't believe in witches or fairies or any kind of supernatural gobbledygook. It was superstitious nonsense, and I didn't want my little girl exposed to those sorts of tales.

I bought a small house next door to the home of Widow Donner, who had twins—a boy and a girl—just a year older than Matilda. All three children played together during the long summer days and walked to school together in the fall.

I admired Widow Donner—a plain, dark-haired, sensible woman who had shouldered the responsibilities of her dead husband's mercantile after he'd passed and was doing a fine job of raising her two children. She kept an eye on Matilda when I went out hunting and trapping, and in exchange, I provided meat for her table several times a week. I spoke often with Widow Donner over the garden fence while I skinned the day's catch and she hoed her vegetables. We became quite good friends.

Widow Donner knew how I felt about supernatural nonsense, so I was extremely put out the day Matilda came home from school and announced that our neighbor had claimed her cow had been hexed.

"Missus Donner said the cow was cursed by three witches," she said as she placed her lunch pail on the kitchen table, where I was carefully sharpening my hunting knives.

"Matilda, you know there are no such things as witches," I said.

"But Pa, Widow Donner said—"

"Matilda!" I interrupted her sharply. "You know I don't approve of supernatural talk."

"Yes, Pa," she said, closing her pink lips into a tight line of disapproval.

We stared sharply at one another for a long moment, until her mouth drooped in compliance. She sighed reluctantly and went out to do her chores.

I put away my knives and stalked outside, fuming as I walked swiftly through the cow pasture and over to the outbuilding where I skinned deer and smoked meat. Widow Donner's garden lay on the far side of the fence, and sure enough, there she was, calmly hoeing. She wore a blue flowered sunbonnet that brought out the blue of her eyes, and the tendrils of her dark hair curled beside her rosy cheeks. She looked rather fetching, despite the sweat beading her forehead. I was too upset to care.

"Mistress Donner, how dare you talk to Matilda about witches!" I shouted as soon as I was in earshot. "You know I don't hold with talk of the supernatural."

Cary Donner stood up straight and looked at me calmly with her intelligent blue eyes. "I did not speak to Matilda about

THREE FAWNS

witches. She overheard me instructing Daniel and Francine about the best way to care for our hexed cow."

"Hexed cow! Ha! Sick cow, you mean," I cried, infuriated by her calm tone.

"Hexed cow," Cary Donner said firmly. "She stopped giving milk overnight, and today, she started chasing her tail like a dog. She got so dizzy the twins had to tie her up to make her stop. Now, she is banging her head repeatedly against the barn wall."

I blinked in surprise over this description, and my mind whirled with all the possible diseases that could make a cow behave in such a manner. Milk fever? The staggers? I rattled off a whole list, and Cary shook her head after each one.

"Okay, Harry. Explain to me why my cow is trying to talk," she said finally, cutting me off midlist.

"What?" I exclaimed in astonishment.

"She's trying to talk," Cary repeated.

"Woman, you must be mad," I said flatly. "That's impossible."

"See for yourself," she said, gesturing toward the garden gate.

With a goaded glare, I stormed through the gate, past my irritating, if attractive, neighbor and into the barnyard. By the time I reached the cow barn, I was trailed by all three children and the fetching Widow Donner. As I stepped into the barn I heard the lowing of a distressed cow . . . a very strange lowing.

"Feeeeeeeeeeeed me. Huuuuuuuuuungry," mooed the cow. The lowing was followed by the *bang, bang, bang* of her horned head against the back of her stall.

My mouth dropped open, and then I hurried through the door and across the wooden floor to stare over the stall door at Daisy. She butted the back wall with her brown and cream head, then turned to roll an eye at me over her shoulder. The twins had tied a rope around her neck and secured it to the walls on either side with two more ropes to prevent the cow from circling to death. But they were going to have to adjust the rope again to keep her from knocking herself silly on the back wall.

"Huuuuuuuuuuuuuuungry," Daisy bellowed when she saw me at the door. "Foooooooooooooood!"

"That's impossible," I gasped as Daisy started banging her head again.

Beside me, Francine slipped through the open door and went over to the hungry cow. "Help me, Daniel," she called to her brother, and together they pushed the cow away from the back wall and adjusted the rope halter to keep her from banging her head again.

"Here's some hay, Daisy," my daughter chirped, dumping the hay into the manger. Francine had to loosen one of the restraining ropes so Daisy could reach.

"Aaaaaaaaank ooooooooooooou," Daisy lowed through a mouthful.

I turned shocked eyes toward Cary. "What? How? I must be losing my mind!"

"You are seeing what we all are seeing," Cary said. "She has been hexed."

"Come on, Pa," Matilda said kindly, taking my hand. "Missus Donner can fix you a cup of tea, and we'll explain things to you."

Still stunned by what I'd seen, I followed my daughter back to Widow Donner's house, while the twins made sure Daisy was secured in her stall.

Over a steaming cup of tea, Cary Donner explained that she had refused to sell Daisy to the youngest of the Mclean sisters, who lived in the log cabin outside town.

"She's one of the witches!" Matilda said excitedly, bouncing in her chair.

Out of habit, I frowned at her, and then blinked when I remembered what I'd just witnessed.

"I am sure the Mclean sisters can't be witches," I said belatedly.

Surely, they could not be. All three sisters had lovely, golden hair, creamy complexions, and demure ways. Half the men in town were in love with them. I, myself, had hankered after the middle Mclean sister, until the day she'd turned down my offer to carry her parcels out to the wagon when she was shopping in the Donner mercantile. There were six of us fellows hanging about on the porch, hoping to squire the pretty woman to her wagon, and I got the choice position near the door. I was the first man to offer my assistance to the lady, but she refused my offer and chose the handsome blacksmith, instead. After being publicly humiliated in such a fashion, I'd lost interest in the middle Mclean sister and turned back to my hunting and trapping. I'd have to look elsewhere for a mother for Matilda.

Francine and Daniel came banging into the house at that moment. Francine heard my remark about the Mclean sisters and exchanged a meaningful glance with Matilda. "Honestly," said Francine, "Men never believe a pretty woman can be a witch!"

"I believe it," Daniel said mildly.

The boy resembled his mother in looks and character. Frances, as golden as the Mclean sisters, must take after her dead father.

Cary smothered a grin and poured her children hot tea. All five of us devoured the biscuits she'd baked while we discussed the hexed cow.

"So," I said, swallowing a buttery mouthful. "How do we fix Daisy, assuming she can be fixed?"

Cary smiled and rose from the table to pick up a couple of silver spoons from her drawer full of utensils. "That's simple," she said, laying them beside me. "I think you should go deer hunting, Harry. With these."

The next day found me face down beneath a bush, the rain pouring all around me. I had my gun under me to keep it dry, which did not add to my comfort. A constant stream of water was dripping from the rim of my hat and running down my nose. I muttered curses at Cary and her crazy ideas as I waited and waited and waited for three fawns to stroll by. Cary insisted that the Mclean sisters were shape-shifters who took on the form of deer when they roamed the woods.

"I've seen them," she'd said. "When I went to the Mclean cabin to buy herbs, I saw three fawns racing through the underbrush. They ran up to the cabin and pushed through the door. As they entered the house, I saw them changing shape! I didn't want the sisters to know I'd seen them shape-shifting, so I waited five minutes before I walked up to the cabin and knocked. When the sisters answered, there were no signs of any fawns in the cabin."

So, there I lay under a soaking-wet bush holding a rifle full of silver bullets, waiting in the rain for three supposedly magic fawns. If I hadn't looked in on Daisy before I'd left, I would have thought I had imagined the whole thing. But Daisy was even worse today: cross-eyed, heavy and swollen with milk that refused to come out of her udder, and moaning in passable English, "Huuuuuuurrrrt. Oooooowwww!"

There was so much swishing rain and swirling mist that I almost didn't see the first fawn as it stepped into the clearing. I was wringing out my saturated hat when a movement caught my eye. I froze in place and watched the fawn saunter a few feet into the rain-soaked grass and start munching. A moment later, two more fawms followed the first into the meadow. Any of the deer would make a decent meal and a nice spotted pelt to sell. I raised my gun and then hesitated. If they really were women . . . witches . . . whatever . . . I probably shouldn't kill them. I'd just wing one of them and see what happened. I aimed at the closest fawn and fired. The bullet winged the deer in the hind leg, just where I'd aimed. The fawns bolted, with the injured one limping at the rear. I followed them at speed through the meadow, over the ridge, and along the stream. Sure enough, we were heading in the direction of the Mclean cabin. Three minutes brought me to the edge of the clearing in time to see the fawns racing through the front door and transforming into women as they stepped inside. The last woman—the youngest sister—stumbled on her injured leg as she transformed. The eldest sister caught her by the arm and helped her inside, while the middle sister shut the door.

My face went tight and grim as I stepped into the clearing with my rifle of silver bullets. I could no longer deny the existence of witches. Cary was right. I walked up to the door and pounded on it with the butt of my rifle. I heard whispering inside, and then the middle sister opened the door.

"Why, Harry," she cooed when she saw me, fluttering her long, blonde eyelashes.

I glared at her, and her smile faded. I pushed inside the cabin and looked over at the bed in the corner, where the youngest sister lay. The eldest Mclean was pressing a bloodstained cloth over the injury. The sisters stared at me in fear as I stalked over to the bed.

Turning abruptly to the middle sister, I said, "Take the spell off Daisy. Right now."

I didn't raise my rifle. I didn't have too. She nodded and backed away from me.

I motioned the eldest sister away from the bed and started giving orders. Hot water. Clean clothes. A clean, sharp knife. I tied a tourniquet above the wound to stop the bleeding, while the youngest sister moaned in pain.

"Give her some whisky to drink," I snapped to the middle sister as soon as she finished her mysterious chanting in the far corner of the room.

She obeyed instantly. When the materials were ready and the youngest sister had drunk enough whisky to relax and blot out some of the pain, I removed the silver bullet from her leg and then cleaned and bandaged the wound. When I finished, I sat back on my heels and somberly regarded the three beautiful sisters.

"I will give you one day to leave town," I said quietly. "If you leave now and remove any spells you've put on the townsfolk, I will not betray your secret. If you don't leave . . ." I didn't finish the sentence.

The sisters sighed almost in unison. "We will leave," said the eldest. "We will leave."

Rising to my feet, I shouldered my rifle and walked to the door.

"Thank you, Harry Belton," the youngest sister said.

At the doorway, I paused for a moment and gave a tiny nod. Then I stepped outside and into the drizzle. As I walked away from the witch cabin, the sun came out, dazzling my eyes with sparkles.

Just as I reached the end of the path, the middle sister called through the window, "Harry, you should marry Widow Donner. She is the reason I refused your offer to carry my packages."

I whirled around, but not in time. The window slammed shut before I could speak. The middle Mclean sister waved happily at me and drew the curtains.

Francine and Daniel ran to meet me when I entered the rain-washed farmyard. Matilda squealed from her place on top of the fence and jumped into my arms.

"Daisy is better, Pa!" she cried. "Did you kill the fawns?"

"I didn't kill them, but I did persuade them to leave town," I said, raising my voice so Cary Donner could hear me from the door of the house.

Cary smiled at me, her blue eyes blazing with the same strong emotion that was coursing through my blood. I smiled back and hurried to meet her. Francine took my free hand in hers as we all walked in a cluster over to the farmhouse.

I wondered, in that moment, if the Mclean sisters had set me up for this moment. Had they truly put a curse on Daisy, or had they just been matchmaking? I realized I didn't care, so long as I could persuade the Widow Donner to marry me.

A sudden movement by the fence caught my eye. A single spotted fawn stood watching us, ears alert, eyes warm. Then, it leapt sideways and was gone.

20

Tom Morgan's Dream

I can't say as I was prepared for what I found in the woods that day. I was mending oyster boats down by the Port Fulton docks one morning 'round about July of 1847, when I found myself running a bit short of wood. So I trotted off into the nearby forest, looking for a tree or two I could lumberjack for spare parts. I hadn't gotten very far when I stumbled over a mound of newly turned dirt, poorly concealed by leaves and other detritus. As I righted myself, I realized that the tip of a shoe was sticking up out of the ground . . . with a foot still in it.

Well, I didn't stick around in those woods. No, sir! Not with a corpse in residence. I ran back down to the docks to report the matter to the authorities. I led the police to the place where I'd stumbled over the body, and they excavated until they uncovered the corpse of a businessman with his skull bashed in. The officers took the body away and put it on display at the market house, asking folks for help in identifying the poor man.

It took a while, but finally a fellow who owned a boardinghouse over in Louisville identified the man as one of his boarders who'd disappeared a few days before. Apparently, the murdered man, whose name was Foxworthy, had gone off

TOM MORGAN'S DREAM

hunting with a bloke named Whittinghill from the same boarding-house. In the morning, Whittinghill had left the boardinghouse with Foxworthy and a fancy hickory club he'd had custom-made.

In the evening, Whittinghill had returned to the boardinghouse without Foxworthy or the club. Whittinghill had spun a spurious story about Foxworthy suddenly deciding to take a job here in Jeffersonville. He had even produced a letter, supposedly from Foxworthy, instructing the landlord to turn over Foxworthy's trunk and other belongings to Whittinghill.

The fellow running the boarding house was mighty suspicious of that letter. He didn't think the handwriting in the letter looked anything like Foxworthy's handwriting. He refused to turn over the trunk to Whittinghill, knowing it contained a large sum of money that Foxworthy had saved up over the years.

"Then, Whittinghill did a runner," the owner of the boardinghouse told the police. "Disappeared without a trace. I knew something suspicious had happened. Poor Foxworthy!"

The police went on a manhunt and soon had Whittinghill in their custody. But the murder weapon was still missing, and without it, the police had no case. The authorities formed a search party to look for it, and I volunteered. I felt I had a vested interest in the case, having found poor Foxworthy in the woods. It was a frustrating search. There were too many nooks and crannies and too much undergrowth in the forest and not enough searchers. For a while, it looked like Whittinghill would get away with murder.

Then, one morning I bumped into a bloke name Tom Morgan who'd been in the search party, same as me, helping the police scour the woods around Jeffersonville for the murder weapon. Tom looked real pale and distressed. I asked what was wrong, and he told me he'd had a strange dream in the middle of the night. In his dream, the ghost of Foxworthy had appeared and led him into the woods. They'd walked a long way, until they reached a swampy area. There, Foxworthy's ghost showed Tom the custom-made hickory club hidden underneath a rotting log.

"I'm sure I'd know the place again if I saw it," Tom told me. "It's a long shot, but I want to try to find it. Will you come with me?"

I agreed at once. I felt I owed it to poor Foxworthy.

Invigorated by this possible clue, we went hunting for the place revealed by the ghost in Tom's dream. We scoured every swamp region within a couple of miles of Jeffersonville. I was about to give up when Tom came running over a small ridge and waved to me, shouting, "This is it! I found the place!"

I ran to join him, and he pointed down into a swampy nook with a rotten log lying near the water. "There's the log I saw in the dream," Tom said.

Tom grabbed a long stick and poked it underneath the rotting log. It hit something hard. Carefully, he pushed the object until it rolled out from under the log. It was a custom-made hickory club, just like the one Tom had seen in his dream. I gasped and clamped a hand over my mouth when I saw it. It was still spattered with blood, brains, and hair from Foxworthy's head.

Whittinghill was convicted of the murder of Foxworthy based upon the witness of the proprietor of the boardinghouse and the evidence Tom had found. The convicted murderer was given the death penalty, but he died a few months before it was carried out, some say of remorse.

So justice was done after all, thanks to Tom Morgan's dream.

21

Strange Case

SOUTH BEND

It was by far the strangest case I'd ever dealt with during my twenty-plus years as a physician serving the town of South Bend. It was 1880, and business was booming, what with all the births, deaths, cuts, scrapes, colds, fevers, and such that make up a daily medical practice. There was also the more tragic side of doctoring, including a particularly sad case of tuberculosis that I'd handled recently. Young Sarah Platt had died of the disease a few months earlier, and I felt her loss keenly. I'd done everything medically possible, to no avail. We had to find a cure for tuberculosis. It killed too many of our young people!

Doctors see the tragic side of life all the time, but I really wasn't prepared when Gordon Truesdale, a local farmer with a wife and four girls, came to my office one day and asked me whether a man might be poisoned from handling a corpse. I was speechless for nearly a minute. What a bizarre question to ask someone—even a doctor—out of the blue. If he were a mortician, it might make more sense. But he was a farmer . . . a very pale and trembling one, I noted, with a feverish flush on his cheeks and too bright eyes.

"Yes. Most definitely," I said belatedly, when I'd recovered from my shock.

"Oh," Gordon said softly, looking at the floor and losing the remainder of his color.

"Why do you ask?" I queried, staring at him long and hard.

"No reason," Gordon said hastily, still looking anywhere but at me. "Just curious."

He rose hastily, muttered "good day," and rushed from my office. As the door slammed shut behind him, I remembered that Gordon was an amateur phrenologist—a very bad one. He liked to feel the bumps on people's heads to analyze their personalities. I'd once heard him boast about his collection of skulls that he used in his "research." Had Gordon been digging around in places God had not intended man to delve? The thought disturbed me so much that I went to the pump and washed my hands vigorously before calling in my next patient.

The very next person in my office was the wife of the local ferrier, whom I was treating for a bad tooth. She was a cousin of the late Sarah Platt, and she had a disturbing tale to tell.

"I suppose you heard about the scandal, doctor?" she asked me as she trudged in the door.

When I replied in the negative, she told me about the jawbone a farmer had found in his field, which was adjacent to the local graveyard.

"It were a human jawbone," the woman said, taking a seat at my gesture. "Turned out to belong to my poor cousin Sarah. Someone dug up her grave and stole her head. Disgraceful! People have no respect for the dead!"

Stole her head? My eyes widened in shock, and my thoughts went instantly to the amateur phrenologist who wanted to know if a person could be poisoned by a corpse. As I examined the painful tooth, I asked for more details and learned the grave had been disturbed sometime in the last two weeks. Not long ago then. And now the amateur phrenologist was feverish and appeared ill. Hmm.

Three days later, Mrs. Truesdale sent her eldest daughter to fetch me; her husband was seriously ill and needed a doctor. I packed my bag, summoned several attendants to aid me in the event surgery was needed, and drove my carriage to the Truesdale farm, wondering what I would find. Gordon abed with fever, perhaps?

When I entered the bedroom where the stricken man lay, I was not prepared for the sight that met my eyes. Gordon's face was so red and swollen, he no longer resembled a human being. His eyes looked as if they might pop right out of his face, but they were turned so far inward with pain that the whites showed. The area across his nose and forehead seemed to have filled with some kind of liquid substance that wobbled slightly whenever he took a breath, which he could do only through his mouth. His lips were drawn back into a snarl of agony, showing what remained of his yellowing teeth.

The smell in the room turned my stomach, and only years of working with the foulest patient conditions kept me calm. Some sort of massive *erysipelas*, I thought, as I took in his symptoms, though I had never seen a case such as this. Perhaps it was a new sort of disease. Whatever was poisoning his system, the only chance I had of saving his life was to get rid of the substance liquefying his body from underneath his skin.

I was glad I'd brought attendants with me, because it was obvious I had to operate immediately. I sent the poor man's wife away. She was nine months pregnant with their fifth child, due to give birth any day. To have a deathly ill husband to tend at the same time was taking a toll on the poor woman, who also had a farm and four young daughters to care for.

We put the man under with chloroform, perhaps the greatest invention of the century, and I made two incisions—one from nose to hairline and the other straight across his forehead— hoping to clear out whatever liquid was building up there before it crushed his brain. Instantly, a viscous, putrescent liquid gushed out of the incisions, filling the room with a smell so foul that several attendants fled the room and the brave man who remained threw up in the corner several times. I stuck grimly to my task as the horrible liquid poured into the large bowl I held up to Gordon's face.

"Get me another bowl!" I snapped to my remaining attendant, not wishing any of the liquid to splash on me and thanking God I'd taken the precaution of wearing gloves.

The swelling in Gordon's face was slowly decreasing as the liquid spewed out, but it was obvious I was going to have to make several more incisions around the man's skull. The attendant brought me a fresh bowl and carried the other bowl out of the house to bury it. When the gush was over, I lightly bandaged the incisions and shaved the poor man's head. Then, I made several more incisions across his skull and went through the same foul process again and again, until the patient's head was roughly the same size as formerly.

"How can a man live through this?" the attendant murmured.

He can't, I thought. *This is what comes of desecrating the dead.*

STRANGE CASE

"We've got to clean out the rest of that mess," I said briskly, doing my best to ignore the gruesome nature of the task.

I injected water into the incisions on his face, and it squirted right through his skin and burst out of the incisions on the rest of his skull. There was obviously no flesh or muscle left inside his skin, nothing under there but bone. I was amazed he was still breathing.

I sewed up Gordon as best I could, and then we cleaned up the befouled bedroom before we brought him around. When his missus had returned to his bedside, I told them both that Gordon would probably not live out the week.

"I'm sorry," I said. "We've done everything we could, but the infection has gone too deep. I will leave an attendant here to help as much as we are able."

"Thank you, doctor," Mrs. Truesdale said bravely.

After motioning for the attendant to leave them alone for a few moments, I went out to the yard to divest myself of my fouled clothing. As I washed under the pump, fearing I would never be cleansed of the putrescent liquid that had oozed from Gordon's body, I heard the couple talking through the open window. In a gasping voice, Gordon confessed his crime to his wife. He had, indeed, dug up the grave of Sarah Platts and stolen her head to aid him in his study of phrenology. He'd tossed away the jawbone on his way home, not needing it for his studies. At the time of the robbery, he'd had an open wound on his nose, and he'd wiped his face with his corpse-befouled hands, unconsciously infecting himself with the disease that was now racing so fatally through his body.

As I straightened up from the pump, soap in hand, I heard Gordon tell his wife that the head was hidden in the barn and should be returned to the Platt family. I bundled my jacket and gloves into a spare blanket and threw them into the back of the carriage.

Once home, I burned my clothes along with the blanket. My wife heated water on the stove, and I scrubbed my skin until it was raw to rid myself of any vestiges of that terrible disease.

Gordon lived—if you could call it that—for three more days. I had attendants with him constantly, and I dropped in whenever I could to monitor his condition. Gordon was rotting from the inside out. The swelling returned as various parts of his body turned to ooze underneath his burning skin. His breath grew so foul and hot that it was impossible to wait on him properly. One attendant whose hand came within six inches of the man's mouth during a routine procedure gave a shriek and leapt away, claiming his skin stung as if he'd fallen in a field of nettles. The odor of decay stayed on the attendant's hand for hours. After that, I ordered anyone attending Mr. Truesdale to wear gloves.

The corrosion of Gordon's flesh continued until his eyes rotted away in their sockets and he could no longer see. His skin was so atrophied that a touch would have caused it to fall from his bones. And the smell was so pervasive that I sent the family to a neighbor's house until the house could be fumigated.

I'd instructed the attendants to clap the man into a coffin as soon as the end came. I was taking no chances on anyone else catching the disease that had done in Gordon. I wanted him buried as quickly as possible. It seemed sacrilege to treat him so disrespectfully, but what else could I do? There were young children and a pregnant mother living in this house, and I was also responsible for the health of the nursing attendants in my service.

As soon as Gordon breathed his last, the attendants picked up the sheet—being loath to touch him—and lowered him into the coffin. Then, they nailed it shut and called for a wagon to take them to the cemetery. Everyone involved had prepared for the rapidness of Gordon's burial, and an open grave lay in wait for its new resident.

Unbeknownst to the attendants, the corpse was swelling with noxious gases inside its new resting place. As the wagon pulled into the yard, the lid of the coffin blew off, and foul air swept over everyone. Coughing and swearing, the valiant attendants recovered the coffin's lid and strapped it down over the swelling corpse. Then, the coffin was loaded into the wagon, which jounced and trounced over the rutted road, heading at speed toward the graveyard.

The attendants and mourners had barely reached the cemetery before the lid exploded from the coffin once more. Noxious fumes poured over the assembly, and the corpse swelled visibly before the eyes of the assembled. The coffin was hastily lowered—lidless—into the open grave, and the mourners stepped back as far as they could while the grave was filled in. When the hasty funeral was complete, everyone went home—except for the Truesdales, who stayed that night with a neighbor, since the air in their house was unbreathable, even after fumigation.

Gordon's fifth daughter was born in the neighbor's home the day after her father, the phrenologist turned grave robber, died.

I paid Gordon's attendants top dollar for that particular assignment, and I hoped to God there were no more grave robbers in town. One case was enough for me.

22

Black Widow

I suppose it isn't proper to dislike your neighbors, but I did not care for Widow Sorrenson, not one bit. Her name was Belle, which did not suit her at all; she was a plain, heavy-set woman who had immigrated to the United States from Norway. Belle moved into a hog farm near our place in November of 1901, bringing with her three girls—her own two daughters and a pretty niece named Jenny Oleson.

Of course, I dropped over with a bit of baking to welcome Belle and the girls to the neighborhood when they first moved in, a standard custom in our community. The widow welcomed me without enthusiasm and offered me a cup of tea. We spoke stiltedly for a polite half hour. She told me she had been married to a Norwegian man in Chicago, and they had owned a confectionary store until it was destroyed by fire two years before.

"My life, it has been filled with tragedy," Belle sighed, wiping tearless hard eyes with a lace-edged handkerchief.

Belle and her husband had collected insurance on their lost business, which had allowed them to keep their home. They had boarded foster children to supplement their income.

"Then, my husband, Mads, passed on—a sudden cerebral hemorrhage. I was in shock," Belle said. "Fortunately for me and the children, Mads had two life insurance policies when he passed, which left us enough money to live on. I felt at the time that the city was not the place to raise a family, so we traded our property in Chicago for this farm. It is better, I feel, for the girls to live in the country."

She nodded to the silent children, playing listlessly in the corner.

I was more than happy to end the conversation when the obligatory thirty minutes had passed. This hard-eyed woman and her spiritless children were not to my taste. Widow Sorrenson's feigned grief and all her talk about insurance made me feel dirty. I went right home and heated up water for a bath, even though it was the middle of the week. I wanted the touch of that house off my skin.

Belle might not have been to my taste, but she managed to land a husband right quick. Within a few months, she was Mrs. Peter Gunness, and her new man dug in and started running the hog farm for her. They seemed happy together, and the children perked up with this addition to their family. All seemed well at the hog farm . . . until the day little Jenny Oleson, who was close friends with our son, came running into our farmyard, crying bitterly.

According to Jenny, her new uncle had been in a terrible accident. She hadn't seen it herself, but her Aunt Belle said that Peter had knocked a pot of boiling water off the stove onto his head and face while bending over to collect his shoes. He'd stood up in a daze of pain, knocking his burnt head against a shelf beside the stove and bringing a sausage grinder down on top of himself.

"He's dead," sobbed Jenny. "Just like Uncle Mads."

I hugged the poor child. What could I say? She'd lost two father figures in the last two years. My son patted Jenny shyly on the shoulder, comforting her as best he could. I couldn't help thinking, as I sat the trembling girl down at the table for cookies and milk, that Belle Gunness probably had a new insurance payment coming to her. The thought made my skin crawl, and I pulled my shawl tighter around me. I couldn't believe I'd just had such a terrible thought.

But I wasn't the only one suspicious of Peter Gunness' sudden, bizarre death. The coroner held an inquest, but the evidence was inconclusive, and the newly widowed Belle Gunness walked free. That day, I told my son that Jenny Oleson was welcome at our house, but I did not want him visiting her at the hog farm.

Belle got herself a hired man named Ray Lamphere to help her around the farm, and lived quite well off the insurance money for some time. Then, I learned from Jenny, who often came to our house to do her homework with my son, that Belle had started putting matrimonial advertisements in the Norwegian newspapers. She wanted another partner to help her run the farm.

"Auntie is always writing letters in the evening," Jenny said carelessly, taking a large bite of apple pie from the plate I'd laid beside her on the kitchen table. "I think she's gotten some responses to her matrimonial advertisements."

So it seemed. Over the next few years, a number of men came to visit Belle on the farm. None of them lasted very long. I guess Widow Gunness was picky about who should share her prosperous farm. We'd see them squiring Belle around town or driving past our house on their way to visit Belle at her farm. Then, a few days would pass, and they were gone. Jenny claimed that the hired man, Ray Lamphere, made the suitors nervous.

"I think he's jealous of Auntie's beaus. I think Ray is sweet on her," she told us over dinner one evening.

My boy looked up at the word "sweet," and he and Jenny smiled at one another. They were sweethearting a bit themselves at the moment. It was an innocent romance—his pa and I made sure of it—but I figured if they still felt the same way next year, then we'd be having a wedding at our place.

So I was quite disturbed when my boy came home from school one afternoon absolutely distraught. Jenny Oleson hadn't come to class that day, and her cousin Myrtle said it was because Belle had sent Jenny off to some fancy school in the east.

"Widow Gunness doesn't like me sweethearting Jenny," my son moaned, dropping into a kitchen chair. "I know that's why she sent Jenny away. Myrtle said last night Jenny was doing chores and complaining about her schoolwork, and this morning she was gone, just like that! Widow Gunness must have packed her up overnight and put her on the first train out of town."

"You and Jenny weren't fooling around, were you?" I asked sternly, sitting down next to him and taking his chin in my hands. "Did you get Jenny in the family way?"

"No, Mama, I swear I didn't," he said earnestly.

I knew my son. He was telling the truth.

"If I had, we would have told you and gotten married right away. You know that. But I never did more than kiss her, Mama, I promise."

"Well, then," I said. That was that.

BLACK WIDOW

My son relaxed when he saw I believed him. "I'll speak with Widow Gunness and get Jenny's address. Then, you can write to her at her new school," I said firmly. "We'll all write to her, so she won't be homesick."

I did not want to go to Widow Gunness' hog farm. Every time I visited the place, I walked away with my skin crawling and had to take a bath. The very air of the hog farm seemed foul, and it wasn't the muddy pigs that made it that way. We had hogs of our own, and they were cleaner than Widow Gunness, in my opinion. But I'd promised my son, and I was pretty distraught myself over losing the girl I'd pegged as my future daughter-in-law.

Fortunately, I met Widow Gunness in the market the next day, so I took the opportunity to asked her about Jenny. She told me the same story Myrtle had told my son. She didn't like the education Jenny was getting at the local school and had sent her niece east to get better training. When I told Belle that my family wanted to write to Jenny at her new school, she stuck her nose up in the air—she really did—and said she wanted her niece to meet a better quality of people than those residing in La Porte. Then she walked away, leaving me with my mouth hanging open. Of all the nerve! Belle Gunness was a money-hungry, man-mad, social climber! Gah!

As I stormed home to complain to my husband, I realized that my son was right. Belle really had separated the couple from one another. My husband and I discussed the matter at length, but what could we do? Belle was Jenny's legal guardian. We had no claim on her. My son asked Myrtle and her sister, Lucy, if they could give him Jenny's address, but they did not have it. Not a soul from home was writing to that poor young woman, unless Belle was sending her letters, which I doubted.

"Don't worry, son," my husband said. "Jenny knows where we live. She will write to us."

But no letter came, and I wondered whether Belle had threatened Jenny in some way to prevent her from contacting us. I wouldn't put it past her.

Naturally, no one in my household would associate with the Gunness family after that. Of course, I heard rumors about Belle. She had another man come to visit her in January, but he disappeared like all the rest. Then, she got into some kind of a disagreement with her hired hand and dismissed him. So much for Jenny's sweethearting theory, or maybe she had been correct, only the sweethearting had all been on Ray Lamphere's side.

According to rumor, Lamphere started harassing Widow Gunness and threatening her family. Belle lodged a complaint against him with the police, and I guess he backed off some. Not long after that, I saw Belle drive past my house with a strange woman beside her. That was odd. I'd seen Belle driving around with plenty of men and with her children, but this was the first time I'd seen her driving with an unknown female companion. The woman was small and light and dressed in traveling clothes. She made Belle look wide and ungainly. *What a pair,* I thought as I returned to my baking, dismissing the incident from my mind.

As usual, though, the sight of Belle made me think of my poor boy. My son had lost a great deal of weight since Jenny's departure, more than a year ago. I hadn't realized he'd set his heart on their marrying when they were done with school nor how devastated he'd be when he realized, at last, that Jenny wasn't going to write to him. My husband and I both told him we thought Belle Gunness had forbidden her niece to communicate with us, but my son was convinced that Jenny would have defied her aunt if she'd truly cared for him. He hadn't looked at another girl since Jenny left, and he was well on his way to being a cynic about love. I didn't like his attitude much, but how could I blame him? I could and did blame Belle, but I couldn't do anything about that either, except avoid her.

I woke a couple of nights later with the smell of smoke coming in the window, which I left cracked open at night to let fresh air into the bedroom. I nudged my husband awake, and we went to the window to peer out. The sky was ablaze, and we realized that Widow Gunness's home was on fire. All grudges went by the wayside in an emergency. The widow and her daughters needed our help, and we would give it to them. We threw on our coats and boots, sent our son to alert the fire brigade, and ran to help in any way we could.

By the time we arrived, the ground floor was ablaze and flames were threatening the roof. No one could go near that roaring inferno, and anyone still inside was already dead. I felt myself shaking in fear for the girls and their mother.

A neighbor from an adjoining farm told us that he and the new hired hand had brought a ladder to check the upstairs rooms for Belle and the girls when the fire first broke out, but the upstairs rooms were empty. That was strange.

"Empty, at this time of night?" I gasped. "Where did they go?"

"They may have run downstairs, trying to get out," he suggested.

That seemed as good a theory as any.

The firemen flocked to the farm as soon as the alarm was given, but the house was too far gone to save. In the morning, when the fire had died down, the firemen had the grim task of finding what remained of the family. A search of the burnt house proved fruitless, until the men went into the cellar. There, they found four bodies lying on a charred mattress—three of them belonging to children and one to a woman. Bizarrely, the woman's body had no head. After hearing this, the sheriff decided it was not fire that had killed the victims. It was murder—plain . . . and not so simple.

Remembering the complaint brought against Lamphere, the former hired hand was arrested and accused of killing the family and starting the fire. It looked like an open-and-shut case against him. Then, a new player entered the scene.

According to the owner of the market, a man named Asa Helgeleine was in La Porte searching for news about his brother, Andrew, who had disappeared in January after visiting the widow Belle with a large amount of cash in his possession. He had been another matrimonial hopeful, and I dimly remembered seeing a man with Widow Gunness around that time. Anyway, Asa had gone to the sheriff and received permission to search the burnt house for some clue as to the whereabouts of his brother.

"They went to the Gunness place today to look around, but the sheriff didn't find anything," the owner of the market concluded. "Asa was pretty disappointed. He came into the market right after the search and told me he's sure Widow Gunness knew something about his brother's whereabouts. Asa wrote to her inquiring after his brother, and he didn't like the tone of her response. He was planning a visit to La Porte to follow up with her, but now she's dead, and there's no way of finding out what it was she knew."

"I'm sorry to hear that," I said.

Inside, I shuddered a little. I was sure Asa was right. The hard-eyed widow probably had known where his brother had gone. But I wasn't going to gossip about the poor creature now that she was dead. I still didn't like her or how she had treated my son, but the past was the past. I left the store feeling soiled, the way I usually felt when discussing Widow Gunness. I went home and had a bath.

The next day, my husband came home ashen and distraught. I'd been baking all day and hadn't left the farm, so I hadn't heard the news. Earlier in the day, Asa had returned to the Gunness farm with the hired hand and a neighbor, and they'd found his brother's neck and arm buried in a rubbish pit. The sheriff had been summoned, and they had started excavating the hole. While they were examining the contents, he'd noticed another soft spot in the earth a few feet away, and they had dug there, too.

"They found Jenny," my husband said, breaking down completely. "Jenny was in the second hole. She never left La Porte."

I must have fainted. I don't remember much about the rest of that day, except that the doctor came and gave me a dose of something that tasted terrible and put me to sleep for hours. I don't know how long I was ill. It seemed as if every time I woke up, some new horror had been added to the story. More bodies were found. Men mostly, but also the bodies of women and children. Many of the bodies had been dismembered. The sheriff and his men put the remains into the carriage house, which acted as a morgue while the investigation continued.

As word spread about the mass grave on the Gunness farm, sightseers started gathering at the edges of the property.

According to my husband, parents were holding up children to the windows of the carriage house to view the grisly remains inside. Norwegian families who'd lost track of some of their men over the last few years were flocking to La Porte to see if their loved ones were among the victims.

By this time, it was clear that Belle, and not Lamphere, was the perpetrator of the crimes. She lured men to her farm with matrimonial ads, asking them to bring money to invest in the farm, and then she killed them. The police believed she poisoned her victims, and then she and Lamphere would dismember them and bury the body parts around the farm.

Folks in town figured that after the widow discharged her hired man, Lamphere threatened to turn Belle in, and she then threatened to implicate him as an accessory to the murders. The sheriff still believed Lamphere had murdered the widow and her children and burned their house. But others were not so sure. The body of the headless woman was much slighter than that of Widow Gunness, and without the head, it was impossible to identify.

When my husband told me that piece of gossip, I was sipping at a bowl of soup. I put my spoon back into the bowl and stared at him in horror, remembering the woman I had seen riding in the carriage with Belle a few days before the fire. I told my husband about the incident, and later I repeated it to the sheriff. I was not happy with the idea that Widow Gunness might still be alive somewhere.

I recovered my health slowly. When I was better, my husband and son took me to visit Jenny's grave. We held a small family ceremony for the girl we all had loved, and I put flowers by the marker. To my surprise, my son looked much better than he had all year. He was grave and sad, but he'd regained the lost weight, and the cynical lines around his mouth and eyes were gone.

"Jenny loved me," he said when I asked him about it.

I took his hand and that of my husband, and together we walked out of the cemetery.

Lamphere was brought to trial and convicted of arson but acquitted of murder. The jury did not say who they thought the murderer was, but they included a statement saying that they believed the woman found in the basement was Belle Gunness. Lamphere was duly sentenced and put into prison, but he died a year later of liver failure. It was rumored that he died believing Belle Gunness was still alive and out there somewhere.

Black Widow: Stay away from me and mine.

Reflection

I was as excited as a new kitten the day my car arrived—a brand new Ford Model T Town Car. I'd been burning to own one from the moment I'd first seen one tooling around Fort Wayne. After months of scraping and saving, I was now the proud owner of the very latest model.

I dragged my wife out of the kitchen to see our new prized possession. "Look, honey! It has a monobloc, four-cylinder engine," I enthused.

"Speak English, Fred," my wife said with a smile.

"And it has a two-speed and reverse epicyclical transmission," I continued, running my hand over the sleek surface of the car. "I've heard it can reach fifty miles per hour! Just imagine!"

"Don't imagine it," my wife said briskly. "Show me!"

I laughed, helped her into the car, and we took off over the rutted roads and wide-open fields around town. Oh, it was fun! We honked the horn and waved at everyone we met. We were the envy of the town!

I cleared out a section of the barn for my new car and parked it next to our carriage. The horses peered over their stall doors

REFLECTION

and stared in perplexity at the sleek new machine. I laughed and scratched my mare, Chelsea, on the nose.

"Don't worry, girl. You aren't out of a job," I told her.

She nuzzled my arm, hoping for a treat. I reached into my pocket and gave her a sugar cube. Then, I went into the house to regale my patient wife with all the wonders of my new purchase.

I wasn't nearly so keen about the Model T a few evenings later when it stopped abruptly on top of a small hill on my way home from the Grand Dutchess after a Fort Wayne Railroaders minor league baseball game. The engine was smoking, so I figured I had overheated it in my haste to get home in time for dinner.

"So much for the 'most reliable machine in the world,'" I muttered, quoting an old Ford advertising slogan as I got out and opened the hood.

Smoke billowed around me. I coughed and wheezed until the breeze cleared away the smoke so I could see inside. Everything was shipshape. The car was just too hot. I sighed. I would have to wait until it cooled down.

I was in a wooded section of the road, and it was getting dark under the trees. I could feel a nip in the air that told me late summer was giving way to fall. I leaned against the side of the car and looked around me. I'd passed this way only a few times and never really looked at this place. Over to one side of the road, I saw a brick chimney towering over crumbled, blackened walls covered with ivy and brambles. Apparently, someone had lived there once.

The sight of the house made me uneasy. I'd heard stories about a burned-down house on a hill near Fort Wayne. Now, what was it I'd heard? Something about kids being afraid of an old woman? A crow cawed overhead and flew across the road to join its friends. I jumped at the sound and then laughed at my silliness.

The story came back to me all at once. There once was a rickety old woman who lived in an old house on top of a hill. She was herb-cunning and sold love potions to silly girls. Folks called her a witch and avoided her when she came into town to buy groceries. She certainly looked like a witch, with her bent back and gnarled cane. She cackled when she laughed, and she always smelled of herbs and spices. She even kept a black cat that the children in town said was her familiar.

A few years back, the cows in the neighborhood went dry far earlier than they should have, and a frost killed many of the crops. A string of bad luck followed for many of the townsfolk, and then in September, it stopped raining. By late October, people were blaming everything from the drought to their misfortunes on the old woman.

"My farm has been hexed," one of the farmers said at the dry-goods store. "I saw the witch standing on top of the hill and flapping a red wool blanket in the direction of my farm. The very next day, my pig dropped dead."

"The witch spat into my front garden, and all my roses died overnight," a woman said from the counter, where the salesgirl was measuring out fabric for a dress.

"My Sarah Jane, she was ill for a week with a high fever after she stopped to pet the witch's black cat," said a tall woman in widow's black. "I thought she would not survive. It's time we did something about that witch!"

Everyone in the shop agreed. But the sheriff, who'd been listening silently from his seat by the woodstove, cautioned folks at this juncture, saying they shouldn't take the law into their own hands. That calmed folks down a mite, but rumors still raced through town, and they got wilder and stranger as the days passed and no rain fell.

Things came to a head the night of the Autumn Dance. A bunch of hotheaded youngsters who'd too much to drink marched up to the witch's house bearing flaming torches. The old woman screamed at them from an upper window, but her yells only made them angrier. They torched the house with the old woman in it, and as it burned to the ground, storm clouds rolled in, and a heavy rainfall broke the drought. Folks reckoned the spell holding back the rain was canceled out when the witch died in the fire. The official story was that a bolt of lightning hit the old house and started the fire. But anyone who attended the Autumn Dance knew that the mob had torched the place.

I shuddered a bit and shifted my weight, my eyes on the chimney, barely visible through the trees. That happened some time ago. I wasn't sure whether it was a true story or just folklore. I wasn't sure I believed in witches.

I checked the engine again, but it was still too hot to turn over. I decided to poke around the old house to see if it was the one from the old story or just an abandoned outbuilding owned by a nearby farmer. The crickets chirruped sleepily as I wandered through the brambles and bushes littering the area between the trees. The grass was high here, and I couldn't tell where the old walkway might have been. As I drew near, I could see my reflection in the broken glass of one of the windows. The walls around it were charred black. This house had surely been destroyed by fire.

A movement caught my eye. My skin prickled, and I turned my head to look. I found myself staring at a cracked pane of glass in the far window. Reflected in the glass I saw myself . . . and standing directly behind me, the bent form of a wrinkled crone leaning on a gnarled walking stick. Her eyes glowed red as they met mine in the reflection, and she smiled nastily, showing crooked, yellow teeth with a gap in them. She raised the stick and pointed it at me, and the end glowed with blue fire.

I shrieked and whirled around. There was no one behind me. But I was suddenly struck by a bolt of pure ice that froze my chest and shot right through to my back. I started shaking from head to toe, and my legs went so numb I fell to the ground.

"Leave me alone!" I yelled. "I had nothing to do with it!"

I crawled forward on hands and knees and grabbed a broken piece of burnt wood. I pushed to my feet and waved the wood frantically in front of me. My second wild swing connected with a *thunk* against the air, as if I'd hit something invisible standing in front of me. I screamed in terror, darted around the invisible something, and ran for my car. A second bolt of ice hit my left side, turning my leg to pins and needles.

I fell against the passenger door of the Model T and managed to get it open with trembling hands. I limped into the car, crawled to the driver's side, and released the brake. The overheated car slowly started rolling down the hill. I felt an invisible icy bolt whizz past the back of my head as the car picked up speed.

"I'm leaving!" I shouted over my shoulder.

Suddenly, the car shuddered, and the smell of smoke surrounding the engine was replaced with the metallic tang of ice. The car kept rolling, and I didn't hit the brake until I was back on level ground, the wooded hillside far behind me.

I staggered out of the car, my legs all pins and needles, and checked the engine. It was covered with ice. Gingerly, I brushed off the ice off and started turning the hand crank. The engine started immediately. Sighing with relief, I drove back to my house, swearing I would take the long way home from minor league ballgames from now on. I was never going near that hill again.

24

The Night Shift

INDIANAPOLIS

When I got laid off from my job, my girlfriend, Maria, suggested I take a position as a night watchman or maintenance worker at the old Central State Hospital. Her cousin was working there, doing maintenance around the buildings, and he'd heard there were positions open. I didn't much favor the idea. I'd lived most of my life in Indianapolis, and I grew up hearing stories about Central State Hospital, both before and after it closed.

In 1848, Central State Hospital opened as a hospital for the insane. Conditions inside the facility were pretty grim in the early years. Patients were neglected and abused. The dungeon-like basements were so dark, humid, and foul that one visiting superintendent said they were unfit for life of any kind. Maniacs—lacking light, air, food, and human companionship—raved and howled like tortured beasts. Rotting floors and rough straw mattresses were the norm, and roofs leaked on patients and staff alike. Those who weren't insane to begin with could easily have been driven mad in those conditions.

Things at the hospital didn't improve until 1890, when the state appointed a special committee to investigate conditions there, which resulted in sweeping reforms. Even then, it remained under a cloud. Rumors still abounded regarding neglect, use of restraints, and patient maltreatment, although many of the staff did their best to help patients, despite conditions such as overcrowding, poor funding, and poor training.

By 1970, most of the hospital's Victorian-era buildings had been declared unsound and were demolished and replaced by brick dormitories. But the rumors continued until the hospital was shut in 1994.

"I've heard strange stories about that place," I told my girlfriend. "People say it's haunted by ghosts of former patients."

"Hogwash! I don't believe in ghosts," she said crisply. "My cousin hasn't had any troubles."

"Your cousin wouldn't know a ghost if it came up and introduced itself to him," I replied just as crisply.

Still, I needed a job, and I didn't think a career in the fast-food industry would suit someone of my temperament. So I went for an interview and was hired immediately as a general handyman.

I started off on the day shift, which wasn't too bad. The old buildings were creaky, and there was an air about the place, as if someone were watching you from dark corners, that made my skin prickle. Still, it wasn't too bad. I'd always liked working with my hands, so doing odd jobs suited me very well. The only place I got really creeped out was the catacombs, which seemed to hiss with silent voices while strange shadows flickered across the walls.

Then, my supervisor asked me to switch over to night duty. I didn't like the notion at all. All along, I'd made sure I was done with my work and hurrying through the wrought iron fence surrounding the campus before dusk. I did not want to

THE NIGHT SHIFT

be at Central State Hospital at night. But my supervisor made it very clear that it was change my hours or lose my job. So I agreed to take the night shift.

The very first night I was on duty, I was walking to a repair job with Maria's cousin, who also worked the night shift, when I heard screaming coming from a grove of trees. I jumped a mile and turned toward the sound, ready to run to the rescue. Maria's cousin caught my arm and pulled me to a halt.

"Amigo, it is just a ghost," he said. "Come on."

"A ghost," I gasped. "What do you mean a ghost? A man is screaming out there."

"No one is out there," he said calmly, though I could see his hand was trembling where it gripped his toolbox. "Many years ago, an inmate stoned a fellow patient to death in that grove. Sometimes, the ghost of the victim cries out. Believe me, it is better not to see!"

I felt guilty for walking away from the grove. I felt as if I might have been able to rescue the screaming man if I'd run into the woods. But how do you rescue a ghost?

The screams stopped as abruptly as they started, and the silence over the nighttime grounds was ominous and full of a dark, churning energy. I was glad when we got to the building. But it was even worse there. The air seemed to pulse with half-heard voices, and I swear footsteps followed us everywhere we went that first evening. The night seemed to last forever, and I practically ran out the door as soon as I signed off my shift.

I thought about telling Maria about the ghosts, now that I knew her cousin also believed in them, but my pragmatic girlfriend would probably laugh at me or worse—call me a coward. I wasn't a coward. Of course not. And, I reasoned, Maria's cousin kept working at the hospital in spite of the ghosts, and nothing had happened to him. So I kept on working there, too.

Gradually, I got used to the old hospital at night. If I heard screams or moans, I ignored them, and I wore a special, priest-blessed silver crucifix around my neck, just in case.

About a month after I started working the night shift, Maria's cousin and I were sent down to the boiler room to pull ashes. I hated the boiler room as soon as I set foot in it. It was shadowy and full of columns and corners, and I knew immediately that we weren't alone.

As we worked with our shovels, I heard someone—I think it was a woman—moaning in a corner of the room. I ignored it, as I'd done all the other times I'd heard strange sounds in the hospital. But the sound grew louder and turned to screams. Maria's cousin suddenly jerked upright and stalked toward the corner, holding his shovel in front of him like a shield. I followed reluctantly and shone my flashlight into the dark place where the light did not reach. No one was there.

We went back to shoveling ashes, but I swear I kept seeing shadows out of the corner of my eyes, flicking from column to column. I broke into a cold sweat and shoveled faster. When we finished, Maria's cousin and I ran out of the room so fast that we hit the doorway in the same instant and were wedged together in the frame for a moment. We jockeyed for position, and finally I shoved Maria's cousin through. I followed a second later, and I swear I felt someone push me in the lower back as I exited the door.

I was shaken by the incident and thought about quitting my job. I wasn't sleeping so well during the day, and Maria had commented on the black shadows under my eyes. I still hadn't told her about the ghosts. But I believed in them. Oh yes, I believed.

I was on break a couple of nights later, hanging out with the guys in the old power house, where the boiler room was, when a coworker came rushing up to us. He was white as a sheet and shaking like a leaf in a hurricane.

"What's the matter?" one of the guys asked him.

"I was . . . taking a nap in . . . one of the pump rooms," the man said, his voice pausing in little jerks as he spoke. "And . . . and . . ."

"And?" I prompted.

"Someone was choking me down there," the man gasped, all in a rush. "I could feel hands around my neck, but when I broke loose and turned on the light, nobody was there."

"You're nuts. You were just dreaming," his friend snapped.

"Oh, yeah," the man said, looking him square in the eye. "What about this?"

He pulled aside his collar, and we could all see deep red marks around his neck. It looked as if heavy fingers had pressed into his throat, trying to choke him. Everyone gasped, and I recoiled, grabbing the crucifix around my neck. As the other men pressed him for details, I grabbed Maria's cousin by the arm.

"That's it!" I hissed. "I quit. I don't care if Maria thinks I'm a coward."

I marched out of the building and headed for the gate as fast as my legs would carry me. As I reached the guardhouse, I saw a figure in white hurrying toward the gate in front of me. It glowed faintly. My arms broke out in goose bumps, and I reversed direction, not wanting to walk into the escaping figure. I nearly mowed down a second ghost slipping past the gatehouse behind me. I dodged just in time to avoid being walked through, and then I exited the benighted hospital on the heels of the two phantom inmates who were trying to escape their fate. The ghosts vanished down the street in one direction, and I tore off in the other. Never again, I vowed as I ran for home. Never again!

I told Maria that if she gave me a hard time about quitting, we were through. I guess my girlfriend likes me more than I thought, because she never mentioned Central State Hospital to me again, and she helped me to find a job with a friend of hers who does carpentry. I discovered later that her cousin quit his job a couple of days after I did, and he told Maria in no uncertain terms that ghosts did exist, thank you very much, and he didn't want to talk about it. So I was vindicated—at least in the eyes of my girl—which counts for a lot.

25

Hatchet Man

BLOOMINGTON

She'd had one too many drinks, and her head was pounding when she got up from the bar. "I need some air," she told her college roommate, who was flirting with the cute bartender. "I'm going back to the dorm."

"I'll be along later," her roommate said distractedly, her eyes fixed on the handsome man behind the bar.

The coed headed out into the street, and the fresh night air brought some relief to the pounding in her head. She walked briskly down the road, breathing deeply, enjoying the lovely night and the brightly lit signs and windows around her. Her enjoyment faded when she made her first turn onto a much narrower, darker street. Her headache returned, but this time it was not the drink that induced it. It was fear.

There were warnings all over campus about a Hatchet Man who was supposedly abusing and killing woman in the town. All the girls were warned to walk in pairs and to stay in brightly lit areas if they had to go out at night. She and her roommate were staying in the dorm over Thanksgiving break, and they'd been bored staying inside every night. So they'd decided to go to the bar that evening. But they hadn't intended to stay so late . . . or to walk home separately.

The girl quickened her pace, aware of every dark shadow. Did she hear heavy breathing behind her? She gasped and started to jog, keeping to lighted paths as best she could. Did someone grunt behind her? Were those footsteps jogging along in time with her? She broke into a run, heart pounding fiercely as she ran through the deserted campus and flung herself into the dorm. She pounded up three flights of stairs, down the hall, and into her room, slamming the door and locking it behind her. It was only then, leaning against the door with her heart racing, that she started to feel foolish. There was no sound from the hallway. No footsteps. No heavy breathing. No hatchet breaking through the wood of the door. She'd been a fool.

She staggered to the bathroom to wash up for the night, leaving the door locked behind her. She kept glancing in the mirror to make sure everything was secure. The scene in the mirror was normal. There was no sound in the empty dormitory. Everything was just fine, she told herself.

Then, she remembered that her roommate was still at the bar. She didn't want her roommate to walk home alone, but it would be foolish for the girl to walk alone back to the bar to meet her. Finally, she called security. No one answered the phone, so she left a message for the guard to watch out for her roommate. Then, she called the bar and asked the manager if he would arrange for her roommate to be brought home in a taxi. The music in the background was loud, and she wasn't sure whether the manager had understood her request. But at least she'd tried.

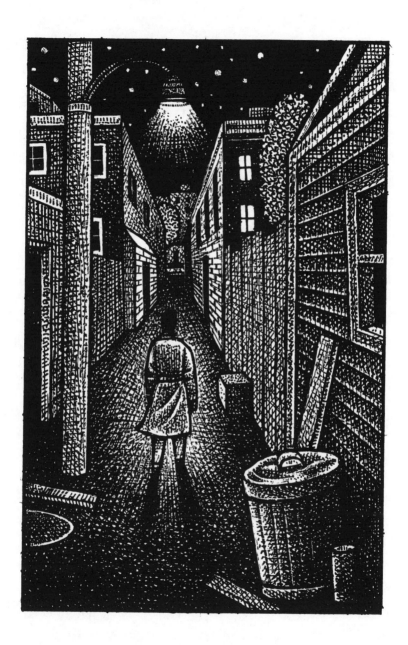

HATCHET MAN

She changed into her pajamas and curled up in bed with the reading lamp on, determined to wait up for her roommate. But the combination of heavy drinking and her earlier fright sent her into a deep sleep almost at once, and she did not awaken until the sun came pouring in the window in the morning.

She groaned when she opened her eyes. She had a hangover, and her current headache was worse than the one she'd had in the barroom the night before. She rolled over, trying not to be sick in the bed, and looked across the room at the bed on the other side, wondering if her roommate was still asleep. Her roommate wasn't there. Moreover, her bed was already made. In fact, it looked as if her bed had not been slept in at all!

She rolled to her feet, heart pounding. Had her roommate come in and left again? She didn't see a note. Maybe her roommate had spent the night in the lobby? She'd done that once before when she was out partying until the wee hours of the morning, saying it was too much trouble to climb three flights of stairs.

With trembling hands, the coed unlocked the door and wrenched it open, poised to race down to the lobby in search of her roommate. She was instantly overwhelmed by the unmistakable, faintly metallic scent of blood that smashed into her nostrils as the door swung open. That was her only warning before her shocked eyes saw blood spattered all over the far wall. She screamed in horror, and her eyes sank toward the floor, which was covered in gore. Her roommate lay at her feet, throat slit from end to end, and pieces of skin were dangling off her arms and legs in strips. Her blue eyes were blank and staring, her mouth twisted in a rictus of pain. Blood pooled under her dead body, and one hand was outstretched toward the door, nails splintered where they had scratched in vain at the wood, trying to summon help from her roommate before it was too late.

The morning sun highlighted every inch of her torn skin and blood-stained dress. But across the center of the body lay a long black shadow. She looked up from her dead roommate in a daze, her gaze following the black shadow to its source. Embedded in the window frame near the entrance to the staircase was a bloodstained hatchet, outlined in the light of the rising sun.

The Hatchet Man had claimed another victim.

Resources

Angelfire.com. "Dogface Bridge." Accessed on
   07/22/2011 at www.angelfire.com/theforce/haunted/
   yourinvestdogface.htm.

———. "Haunted Fort Wayne." Accessed on 09/24/2011 at
   www.angelfire.com/scary/hauntedfortwayne.

Asfar, Daniel, and Edrick Thay. *Ghost Stories of America.*
   Edmonton, AB: Ghost House Books, 2001.

Baker, Ronald L. *Hoosier Folk Legends.* Bloomington, IN:
   Indiana University Press, 1982.

Baker, Tom, and Jonathan Tichenal. *Haunted Indianapolis
   and Other Indiana Ghost Stories.* Atglen, PA: Schiffer
   Publishing Ltd., 2008.

Battle, Kemp P. *Great American Folklore.* New York:
   Doubleday & Company, Inc., 1986.

Botkin, B. A., ed. *A Treasury of American Folklore.* New York:
   Crown, 1944.

Brunvand, Jan Harold. *The Choking Doberman and Other
   Urban Legends.* New York: W. W. Norton, 1984.

———. *The Vanishing Hitchhiker.* New York: W. W. Norton,
   1981.

Coffin, Tristram P., and Hennig Cohen, eds. *Folklore in
   America.* New York: Doubleday & AMP, 1966.

———. *Folklore from the Working Folk of America.* New York: Doubleday, 1973.

Cohen, Daniel, and Susan Cohen. *Hauntings & Horrors.* New York: Dutton Children's Books, 2002.

Dégh, Linda, ed. *Indiana Folklore: A Reader.* Bloomington, IN: Indiana University Press, 1980.

Dorson, R. M. *America in Legend.* New York: Pantheon Books, 1973.

Downer, Deborah L. *Classic American Ghost Stories.* Little Rock, AR: August House Publishers, Inc.

Erdoes, Richard, and Alfonso Ortiz. *American Indian Myths and Legends.* New York: Pantheon Books, 1984.

Flanagan, J. T., and A. P. Hudson. *The American Folk Reader.* New York: A. S. Barnes & Co., 1958.

Gendisasters.com. "Hammond, Indiana; Hagenbach-Wallace Circus Train Wreck; June 22, 1918." Accessed on 09/25/2011 at www.gendisasters.com/data1/in/trains/ hammond-circustrainwreck1918.htm.

Geocaching.com. "Old Purple Head." Accessed on 07/03/2011 at www.geocaching.com/seek/cache_details .aspx?guid=48130649-257b-47f2-948d-c04dc749ee47.

Haskell Institute. *Myths, Legends, Superstitions of North American Indian The Life Treasury of American Folklore.* New York: Time Inc., 1961.

Hauck, Dennis William. *Haunted Places: The National Directory.* New York: Penguin Books, 1994.

Holub, Joan. *The Haunted States of America*. New York: Aladdin Paperbacks, 2001.

Homepage.mac.com. "My Adventure on the Troll Bridge." Accessed on 07/02/2011 at http://homepage.mac.com/ dunestrider/Adventure/index.html.

IndyScribe.com. Image of Chain on Haunted Tombstone. Accessed 7/9/11 at www.indyscribe.com/hoosier_ oddities/image_of_chain_on_haunted_tombstone.html.

Kentucky Gazette. "Horror of Horrors." March 24, 1880.

Klockow, Kat. *Haunted Hoosier Halls: Indiana University*. Atglen, PA: Schiffer Publishing Ltd., 2010.

Kobrowski, Nicole R. *Encyclopedia of Haunted Indiana*. Westfield, IN: unseenpress.com, inc., 2008.

———. *Haunted Backroads: Central Indiana*. Westfield, IN: unseenpress.com, inc., 2006.

Leach, M. *The Rainbow Book of American Folk Tales and Legends*. New York: The World Publishing Co., 1958.

Leeming, David, and Jake Pagey. *Myths, Legends, & Folktales of America*. New York: Oxford University Press, 1999.

Life Treasury of American Folklore. New York: Time Inc., 1961.

Long, Megan. *Ghosts of the Great Lakes*. Toronto, Ontario: Lynx Images Inc, 2003.

Louisville Courier-Journal. "Convicted by a Ghost." May 28, 1888.

Marimen, Mark. *Haunted Indiana*. Holt, MI: Thunder Bay Press, 1997.

———. *Haunted Indiana 2*. Holt, MI: Thunder Bay Press, 1999.

———. *Haunted Indiana 3*. Holt, MI: Thunder Bay Press, 2001.

———. *Haunted Indiana 4*. Holt, MI: Thunder Bay Press, 2005.

Marimen, Mark, James A. Willis, and Troy Taylor. *Weird Indiana*. New York: Sterling Publishing Co., Inc., 2008.

McQueen, Keven. *Forgotten Tales of Indiana*. Charleston, SC: The History Press, 2009.

Mott, A. S. *Ghost Stories of America, Vol. II*. Edmonton, AB: Ghost House Books, 2003.

Norman, Michael, and Beth Scott. *Historic Haunted America*. New York: Tor Books, 1995.

Osborne, Stephen. *South Bend Ghosts*. Atglen, PA: Schiffer Publishing Ltd.

Peck, Catherine, ed. *A Treasury of North American Folk Tales*. New York: W. W. Norton, 1998.

Polley, J., ed. *American Folklore and Legend*. New York: Reader's Digest Association, 1978.

Reevy, Tony. *Ghost Train!* Lynchburg, VA: TLC Publishing, 1998.

Rule, Leslie. *Coast to Coast Ghosts.* Kansas City, KS: Andrews McMeel Publishing, 2001.

Sankowsky, Lorri and Kerri Young. *Ghost Hunter's Guide to Indianapolis.* Gretna, LA: Pelican Publishing Company, 2008.

Schwartz, Alvin. *Scary Stories to Tell in the Dark.* New York: Harper Collins, 1981.

Scott, Beth and Michael Norman. *Haunted Heartland.* New York: Warner Books, 1985.

Skinner, Charles M. *American Myths and Legends, Vol. 1.* Philadelphia: J. B. Lippincott, 1903.

———. *Myths and Legends of Our Own Land, Vol. 1 & 2.* Philadelphia: J. B. Lippincott, 1896.

Spence, Lewis. *North American Indians.* Myths and Legends Series. London: Bracken Books, 1985.

Stonehouse, Frederick. *Haunted Lake Michigan.* Duluth, MN: Lake Superior Port Cities, Inc., 2006.

———. *Haunted Lakes.* Duluth, MN: Lake Superior Port Cities, Inc., 1997.

———. *Haunted Lakes II.* Duluth, MN: Lake Superior Port Cities, Inc., 2000.

StrangeUSA.com. "Haunt in Bond's Chapel." Paoli, Indiana 47454. Accessed on 07/09/11 at www.strangeusa.com/Viewlocation.aspx?id=3409.

———. "Little Egypt Cemetery." Accessed on 07/02/2011 at www.strangeusa.com/Viewlocation.aspx?id=3189.

Students of Haskell Institute. *Myths, Legends, Superstitions of North American Indian Tribes.* Cherokee, NC: Cherokee Publications, 1995.

Thay, Edrick. *Ghost Stories of Indiana.* Auburn, WA: Lone Pine Publishing International, 2002.

Toddatteberry.com. "The Ghost of Purple Head Bridge (Stangle's Bridge), Between St. Francisville, Illinois and Vincennes, Indiana." Accessed on 07/03/2011 at www.toddatteberry.com/The-Midwest/Vincennes-Indiana/7051531_XuzoR/2/368132603_Qb2V7#368132603_Qb2V7.

Willis, Wanda Lou. *Haunted Hoosier Trails.* Cincinnati, OH: Clerisy Press, 2002.

———. *More Haunted Hoosier Trails.* Cincinnati, OH: Emmis Books, 2004.

YouTube.com. "Dog Face Bridge." Accessed on 07/22/2011 at www.youtube.com/watch?v=ob2P17bLaX8.

Zeitlin, Steven J., Amy J. Kotkin, and Holly Cutting Baker. *A Celebration of American Family Folklore.* New York: Pantheon Books, 1982.

About the Author

Author S. E. Schlosser has been telling stories since she was a child, when games of "let's pretend" quickly built themselves into full-length stories. A graduate of the Institute of Children's Literature and Rutgers University, she also created and maintains www.AmericanFolklore.net, where she shares a wealth of stories from all fifty states, some dating back to the origins of America.

About the Illustrator

Artist Paul Hoffman trained in painting and printmaking. His first extensive illustration work on assignment was in Egypt, drawing ancient wall reliefs for the University of Chicago. His work graces books of many genres—including children's titles, textbooks, short story collections, natural history volumes, and numerous cookbooks. For *Spooky Indiana,* he employed a scratchboard technique and an active imagination.